THE GORKHA GRIEF

THE GORKHA GRIEF

Tim I Gurung

Vitasta

Published by
Renu Kaul Verma
Vitasta Publishing Pvt Ltd
4348/4C, Ansari Road, Daryaganj
New Delhi – 110 002
info@vitastapublishing.com

ISBN 978-81-19670-31-4
© Tim I Gurung
First Edition 2024
MRP ₹ 495

All Rights Reserved.
No part of this publication may be reproduced, stored in a retrieval system, or transmitted in any form, or by any means—electronic, mechanical, photocopying, recording or otherwise—without the prior permission of the publisher. Opinions expressed in it are the author's own. The publisher is in no way responsible for these.

Edited by Anuradha Mukherjee
Cover and layout by Rohit Gautam
Printed by Vikas Computer and Printers, New Delhi

Contents

Preface	*vii*
Introduction	1
The Indian Gorkha Brigade	14
The Gorkhas in Assam Rifles and other Service Corps	35
The Gorkhas in the Garhwal Divsion	40
The Gorkhas in Sikkim, Darjeeling, Kalimpong, and Bhutan	50
The Gorkhas in the Northeast	58
The Gorkhas in New Delhi and other Parts of India	69
Vying for Autonomy—The Gorkhaland Movement	74
The Inevitable Impact on the Gorkha Community	89
The Bhutanese Refugee Crisis	97
The Implications of the Indo-Nepal Treaty 1950	105
The Gorkha's Loss of Identity	113
The Stigmatisation of the Gorkha	122
The Gorkha Justice Campaign	130

The Nepal Situation	137
The Chief Architects of the Gorkha Grief	153
The Position of the Nepali Elites	163
How Does Nepal View India?	174
The Roles and Responsibilities of the Nepali Leadership	183
The Gorkhas' Future	193
The Gorkha Grief	204
Acknowledgements	*217*

Preface

After the publication of *Ayo Gorkhali—A History of the Gorkhas* in 2020, I received several messages and comments through social media, newspapers, and personal notes, and most comments were positive. Still, one particular comment grabbed my attention and stuck in the back of my mind for quite some time. It came from a group of scholars and intellectuals in India, and they all had the same grievances—despite having a chapter on the Indian Gorkhas, they complained that the book did not cover enough of the Indian Gorkhas. *Ayo Gorkhali* covered the British Gorkha side of history and adding more on the Indian Gorkhas was not the book's scope, therefore, I moved on.

Then, the pandemic struck, bringing the entire world to a grinding halt. Ravaged by the prolonged pandemic and confined within its border, I needed a break and jumped on the first opportunity to get out of my home country. I had been thinking of my next move invariably for the last two years which helped make my decision more manageable, so I was ready when the opportunity eventually came knocking. Since I had started this Gorkha saga, the onus was on me to finish it, and my job would not be complete without the inclusion of the Indian Gorkhas. *If I combined both the army and the civilians from the Indian Gorkhas, I could already have a book by itself,* I thought and made up my mind. I decided to write about the Indian Gorkhas as my second and last Gorkha book. All I had to do then was to pack my bag, visit those places, and meet as many Indian Gorkhas of Nepali origin as possible.

It was late May 2022 when I finally took a plane and embarked on my fact-finding trip. The three-month journey took me to various parts of Nepal and India. I visited India's Dehradun, Haridwar, Nainital, Siliguri, Darjeeling, Gangtok, Kalimpong, Guwahati, and Meghalaya and met hundreds of people with different backgrounds from both sides of the border. I purposefully arranged my trip through the northwestern and northeastern parts of India, where most of the Indian Gorkhas have been residing for ages, and I did not travel to other parts of India. I met scholars, intellectuals, politicians, students, professors, community leaders, social workers, doctors, religious leaders, business people, army and police officers, and ordinary folks like farmers, shopkeepers, taxi drivers, and house-makers. Still, they all had one thing in common—whether they had been residing in Nepal or India, they were all people of Nepali/Gorkhali origins.

After talking with hundreds of my fellow compatriots in both Nepal and India, I have learned a great deal that has changed my whole perception of them. This book is about my genuine and honest views and feelings for them.

Since I had been living most of my adult life outside Nepal, I needed to understand my country first. I spent the first month of my trip in Kathmandu, meeting as many people as possible. I met people from all walks of life, rich and powerful, intelligent yet humble, ordinary and kind folks, educated but with a little bit of attitude, and people full of dreams, ambitions, and aspirations. I met people from the high, middle, and bottom tiers of society, and learned much from everyone. In the end, I realised that most of the things they said sounded more familiar to me, and I felt like I had somehow already known them. After all, they were my fellow countrymen, and I was one of them. I could intuitively feel the country's pulse, and all I needed was just the confirmation of what I had already known or felt. Still, I was genuinely grateful to them for taking the time to come and talk to me and making me feel welcome.

You cannot get the pulse of a country only by visiting Kathmandu alone, for there are different places and people. But let me tell you this—Kathmandu is where all the powers are, and everything about the country happens here. What's more, I have visited many parts of the country during my previous project and have a general idea of what the country looks like.

My visit to India started with a mix of excitement and apprehension, for it was my first-ever trip to India, and it did not go as planned. When we arrived at Dehradun, we had a rough start and the hotel, food, and services were different from what we expected. Surrounded by unfamiliar faces in a new place, I found it quite intimidating. Yet my biggest issue throughout our visit to India was not getting a spot for your morning tea or a quick breakfast before ten, which was annoying for me, as someone who had access to almost anything 24/7. Maybe the hotels we had stayed in were too common, but I needed to gain experience to make any comparison.

Our situation improved after meeting with Nepali locals, who were kind, helpful and welcoming. After meeting community leaders, intellectuals, and other dignitaries, I forgot about my daily problems and started paying attention to my work. We headed to Nainital after visiting the famous Khalanga Fort and other historical places in Dehradun. I could fully relax and enjoy the trip only after we arrived in Siliguri, the first stop of our journey in the northeastern part of India, where I felt like we hadn't left Nepal at all. From there on, everybody we met, talked to, and associated with for the rest of our trip were all people of Nepali origin, and we conversed in Nepali as if we were back in Nepal. We then completed our remaining trips to Darjeeling, Gangtok, Kalimpong, and Guwahati/Assam smoothly without any problems.

The highlight of the entire trip for me, however, was when we visited a Nepali village at the border between Assam and Meghalaya, where every villager was a cow herder. This profession has stayed the same for the last two hundred years. My three-month-long research trip to Nepal and India was an eye-opener, I learned a lot about my people, and every bit of it was worthwhile.

In search of a better future, we Nepalis have had an ancient tradition of going outside the country for over two centuries. The trends have not waned at all over these years. It started two centuries ago with soldiering, and then farming, labouring, animal grazing and husbandry, working in mines, roads, railways, tea plantations, and as security guards. Nowadays, Nepali people work in various areas in both blue and white-collar industries, just as people from other countries have travelled to almost every country of the world. Due to a lack of job opportunities, uncertain future, bad governance and corruption, and unfairness and cronyism back at home, our youths are forced to leave the country for a better chance outside. A long queue in front of the departure gate in the Kathmandu airport has become a familiar scene for all to see.

Due to its geographical position (India surrounds Nepal on three sides, and the Himalayas block the north), India has always been the first and the only option for Nepali migrant workers, and migrating to India has become a tradition for over the last two centuries. Thousands of Nepali youths still join the Indian Army yearly to continue the two-hundred-year Gorkha tradition that started in 1815. Groups after groups of young men walked down the hills of west Nepal, crossed the Mahakali River, and worked in lowly paid jobs in places like Pithoragarh, Almora, Nainital, Dehradun, and other parts of northwestern India. Different groups of young men from mid-western and southern Nepal have headed down to Lucknow, Gorakhpur, Kanpur, Patna, and other parts of Bihar and Uttar Pradesh. Men from the hills of east Nepal have crossed the borders at Kakarvitta and Pashupati Nagar. They arrive at Siliguri, Darjeeling, Kalimpong, Gangtok, and further East to Guwahati, Shillong, Manipur, Nagaland, and the Burmese border.

Children of Nepali elites flooded mainly to Varanasi, Kolkata, New Delhi, and Mumbai for study. Most of those Nepali elites had a connection with those rich and powerful people from India and kept properties there as insurance. Political outfits from Nepal gathered in Varanasi, and Nepali Brahmins came down to attend Sanskrit universities in Varanasi. Sons of ordinary folks came down and went wherever the journey took them to their next job. They worked as manual workers, shop assistants, security guards, construction workers, drivers, servants, porters, etc. Estimated to be over a million Nepalis working in India at a time, many Nepali families, communities, and villages in Nepal still rely on these jobs for their survival.

Migrating to India was made possible by *The Indo-Nepal Treaty of Peace and Friendship* signed between India and Nepal in 1950, which allowed citizens from both countries to enter, work, and buy property in the other country in a reciprocal way. People from both sides have taken advantage of the open border policy since then. Events in the last few decades have changed people's views, and so has globalisation and Information technology (IT), as people have become more aware of their rights, security, and identity. The escalation of The Gorkhaland Movement, The Assam Movement 1979-1985, The Bodo Movement, and The Bhutanese Refugees Crisis also deeply impacted the Gorkhali communities in Northeast India. They suddenly realised they could be displaced overnight from the land they had taken as their only home for generations. The open border policy also created an unprecedented rift between the Nepalis on both sides of the border. It started an identity crisis that would become the focal point of the never-ending debate within the Gorkhali communities. Eventually, there's come a time when they have to give proof of their identity to a place they have been calling home for centuries. Why? They asked, and the question became louder and louder without any signs of abating, let alone an answer.

It has been over two centuries since we, the Nepalis, have been following this practice of *Muglan Pasne* (crossing the border for a better opportunity). So much so that it has become a tradition and Nepalis live in almost every part and corner of the world today. You name it—Europe, North and South Americas, the Middle East, Russia, North and East Asia, Africa, Australia, and Oceania countries—and you will find Nepalis there. According to the government's record, Nepalis have migrated to 153 out of 195 countries of the world, and at this pace, they will soon see themselves in each country of the world.

In my recent stay in Kathmandu, I was lucky enough to meet hundreds of people, and they represented all three tiers of society—high, middle, and low. Still, they all had one thing in common, which is that they were all associated with a foreign embassy, INGO, or an institution. The building in the central city areas was plastered with posters, advertisements, and coaching centres for the opportunity of migrating to a foreign country. Every youth with confidence, education, and courage dreamt about relocating to a foreign country as if they had already lifted one foot off the ground. And that raised a serious question in the back of my mind: perhaps all the Nepali should do the same.

Nepalis have already been working for other people for the last two centuries. It has been too long not working for their own sake. It may be time to stop and think about it. Was it a good idea? What did you get? Were the troubles all worthwhile? What happened to your country, community, and people? Did you get a fair deal? Did your country, society, and people benefit from this? Do you need to rely on foreign aid? Why do you have to go outside to eke out a living? Can't you do that back at home? Who cares for your home if you all go outside the country? Why do you have no job and no industries at home? Why do you have to import almost everything? Why do you produce nearly nothing here at an industrial level? Why are there not enough jobs for your people? Why are there no developments in your country? Why are you lagging in almost every field, such as education, health, and public infrastructure? What happened to your self-pride, honour, and dignity? Why are you still poor? What happened to your country? And who are you?

This may be the right time for all Nepalis to start asking these hard questions themselves and try to find an answer. I have just done it, and this book is the result of what I found out. It does not hold all the answers, but at least I tried to ask all the right questions and gave a name—*The Gorkha Grief.* It's not only about you and me but about us, the Gorkhas/Nepalis, for a single reason—because it's written with the tears of all the long-suffering Nepalis from around the world, and it's our story.

For simplicity purposes, I have used the word Gorkhali to refer to all the people of Nepali origin in India and around the globe, and Gorkha is the standard spelling in India/Nepal.

The book's scope is also not to propagate past movements such as the Assam Movement and Bodo Movement but to highlight the problems the Gorkhas faced during those difficult periods. I also did not write this book to please or offend any individuals, communities, or countries. My sole intention in writing this book is to compile the Gorkha grief and highlight and tell the truth as it is so the Gorkha community and readers alike can find out the truth and appreciate and learn from it.

Last but not least, this is not a historical, academic, or

scholarly book but a compilation of the views of a curious writer whose concerns and care for his people, community, and country are genuine. The primary purpose of this work is purely for the goodwill and well-being of his fellow compatriots.

Introduction

The migration of Nepali workers, commonly known as *Muglan Pasne or Lahure Jaane*, to India, started between the late eighteenth and early nineteenth centuries. It is carried out in two main ways—as a soldier and a civilian. Before coming to that point, let us talk a little about Nepal's background history at that particular time.

Before Nepal's unification in 1767, there were various princely states known as the *Baisse* and *Chaubisse Rajya* spreading along the hillsides of the rugged mountains just below the majestic Himalayas. They had a Newar King, a Magar King, a Gurung King, a Thakuri King, a Shah King, a Rai King, a Limbu King, and many more. Prithvi Narayan Shah, a courageous, farsighted, and ambitious King from the tiny state of Gorkha, managed to create a strong army that would eventually conquer every other state and form a united Nepal. The mighty King died young before he could fulfil his dream, but his descendants picked up from where he had left off and continued his legacy until his dream of having a unified Nepal was finally achieved. The strong army he had created went on to win many battles along the way and became famous as *The Mighty Gorkhali Force*.

By the early nineteen century, the task of forming the greater Nepal was completed, and its border extended from the Teesta River in the East to the Kangra Valley in the

West. Besides the Gorkhali Force, the British, the Sikhs, and the Marathas were the powers in South Asia. They were to cross each other's way sooner than later because the army was operating and being sustained through a Jagiri system in which the army personnel received their reward through newly acquired lands and taxes instead of a fixed salary from the central government. As a result, one was expected to keep on winning and acquiring new lands just to get paid regularly, and that was precisely what happened in 1814 when the British declared war on the Gorkhali army over a land dispute on the South border of Butwal that had been dragging on for some times by then. The first phase of the Anglo-Gorkha War of 1814-16 lasted eight months, and the British came fully prepared with a massive force of soldiers, guns, and other artilleries to confront the mighty Gorkhali army. The famous Gorkhali army didn't disappoint the British either.

After Lord Moira, the then Governor-General of Bengal, declared war on Nepal on 1 November 1814. The British came with 50,000 men and 100 artillery guns to fight the Gorkhali Force, which had only 14,000 men with no guns. The British came in from five different directions. General Ochterlony's division, with 11575 men and 22 guns, assembled at Karnal and Ludhiana to expel the Gorkhas from the western front. General Gillespie's Force of 17090 men with 20 guns was to take Dehradun. General Wood, with 5598 men and 17 guns, assembled at Gorakhpur to bring the Palpa-Riri route to cut the main Gorkha line of control to the west and advance towards Gorkha to assist General Marley. General Marley, with 13424 men and 47 guns assembled at Sarun-Dinapur, was supposedly heading directly to Kathmandu through Hetauda and Makawanpur as the primary attacking force. Captain Latter and his Rangpur battalion came with the order to encourage the Sikkim Army to get involved with the Gorkhas on the eastern front.

Out of the six British Generals involved in the campaign,

one was killed, another was removed, and three reprimanded. The battles took place mainly at the western front, the Khalanga/Nalapani Fort being the most famous one, where Captain Balbadra Kunwar and his 600 men fought bravely and held up the mighty British forces for a month. Despite being under siege for an extended period, the Gorkhas kept going until the enemy cut off the only water supply to the fort. When the British entered the fort, they found only dead and wounded women and children, whereas Captain Balbhadra slipped out under the veil of darkness with his ninety surviving men. General Gillespie died in the battle and was replaced by General Martindell. In respect for the two brave commanders, two white obelisks for Captain Balbhadra and General Gillespie were erected side by side at the hill at the end of the war, which has since become the top tourist destination in Dehradun. During my research trip to India, I had the honour of visiting the historical site personally and appreciated its significance in our history. The good people of Dehradun have erected the Khalanga War Memorial Pillar at the top of the Nalapani hill and preserved the Khalanga monuments at Shahastradhara road for the world to see and learn about Gorkha's bravery.

Despite being outnumbered and outgunned by the British, the Gorkhas fought on to the end, displaying unparalleled bravery and tenacity in several battles. The defeat forced the Gorkhali side to sign a humiliating treaty on 15 May 1815, known as the Sugauli Treaty. Nepal lost most of its newly acquired lands and shrank to more or less the same size as today's Nepal. Nepal Durbar was to ratify the Sugauli Treaty by Christmas the same year, but they dithered, prompting General Ochterlony to advance toward Kathmandu valley via Makawanpur with 14000 men and 83 guns. Rattled by the news of the British troops arriving near Kathmandu, The Nepali Ruler panicked and officially signed the treaty, ending the war on March 1816. The second phase of The Anglo-Gorkha War lasted for a month.

The British achieved its three main goals from the treaty. First, Nepal could never rechallenge the British. Second, they established a British resident in Kathmandu to keep a tab on Nepal. Third, they opened up a trade route to Tibet for its gold.

It took some time for the British to implement the second and third goals, but they quickly found a perfect way to achieve their first goal of making Nepal a toothless tiger, so it could never bite them again. The British were so impressed by the Gorkhas' courage, loyalty, and tenacity that they decided to have the Gorkhas on their side right in the middle of the war. By the time the first phase of the Anglo-Gorkha War ended, they already had five thousand men of irregulars, deserters, and volunteers on their side and started a new Gorkha force with three battalions. The first Nasiri battalion raised at Subathu is now known as the First Gorkha Rifles of the Indian National Army. The second Sirmoor battalion, raised in Nahan, was later known as "Second King Edward VII's own Gorkha Rifles", transferred to the British Army after 1947, and disbanded in 1994. The third Kumaon battalion raised at Almora is now known as the Third Gorkha Rifles of the Indian National Army.

Since Nepal didn't officially sanction the Gorkha recruitment policy before 1886, the British had to use ingenious ways to get their men, for they had already raised five Gorkha regiments within the ranks of their regular Army by then. Young men wishing to join the Gorkha regiment faced discouragement, harassment, and punishment by the authorities. In some cases, they got fined, beaten up, and all their assets confiscated. As a result, one needed a lot of courage and persuasion and had to be smuggled out of Nepal by someone to join the Regiment. Recruiting agents (Gallawalas) representing the Commanding officer and the Subedar Major of the Gorkha Regiments were discreetly sent to Nepal and took more time to return with suitable Gorkha recruits. To solve the pressing issue, the British encouraged the Gorkha soldiers to bring along their families and allowed them to settle near the army camps, which helped spare all those men from constantly worrying about their families and allowed them to pay more attention to their daily jobs. Over time, it became standard practice for the army personnel to bring their young sons to work so they could learn the trade and help carry the loads when needed. They even followed their fathers into real battles and helped carry water bottles, ration bags, and ammunition regularly. They were later known as 'The Line Boys' who went on to win various bravery medals in actual wars, including the Sepoy Munity 1957-58. They became professional soldiers once they reached adulthood and turned out to be some of the best officers and soldiers within the Gorkha regiments.

The authority also encouraged the Gorkhas to stay behind after they retired. To give more prominence and legality, the British issued a charter in 1860, later known as The Gorkha Charter, which allowed the Gorkha community to buy lands, build houses, and raise families in India as locals so that they could create a pool of new blood within the community for the future Gorkha recruitments. Slowly but firmly, a new Gorkha community started popping up around the military cantonments, giving a new meaning to their existence with multiple possibilities within their newly adopted country, India.

After Bir Shumsher officially sanctioned the Gorkha recruitment policy in the British Indian Gorkha Regiments in 1886, Lord Roberts, the then Army Chief with a soft spot for the Gorkhas, visited Nepal and was welcomed with an unprecedented display of pomp and pageantry. After his visit, the floodgate of Gorkhali youths joining the British Indian Gorkha Army fully opened for the first time after 71 years of its inception. By the early twentieth century, the British Indian Gorkha Brigade already had ten Gorkha Regiments with two battalions each, comprising a peacetime force of 20,000 men at a time. That number changed in India's independence in 1947, except during the extraordinary time of both WW1 and WW2.

In The First World War 1914-18 alone, over 200,000 Gorkhas out of five million populations of Nepal went to the war, and about 20,000 didn't return home. Similarly, during World War II, 250,000 men out of six million populations from Nepal fought for the British, and a little over 33,000 men lost their lives. In addition to the ten existing Gorkha Regiments, they added one more—the Eleventh Gorkha Rifles. Each Regiment had five battalions instead of two as it had in peacetime. After the two World Wars, the Gorkha Regiments returned to their peacetime strength and the surplus Gorkhas were relieved from the services and allowed to return home.

After India's independence in 1947, the British left India and headed to Malaysia or Singapore. Four out of ten Gorkha Regiments also went with the British, while the six stayed behind to become a part of the newly formed Indian National Army. The Eleventh Gorkha Rifles, which had been created and disbanded during the First World War, got a new lease of life and has since remained one of the most distinguished Gorkha Regiments in the Indian Army as of today.

The Gorkha institution started in 1815 and is still strong after 207 years. The Gorkhas currently serve in the British and Indian national armies, Singapore Police, and Brunei's security force. More details about the Gorkhas are explained in later chapters. One must remember that the British were not the first ones the Gorkhas had served with. Instead, it was the Khalsa Army of Maharaja Ranjit Singh at Lahore (currently in Pakistan) where the Gorkhas first started, including Captain Balbhadra Kunwor of the Khalanga/Nalapani fame. And that was precisely where they got their nickname—*the Lahures*. The Gorkhas are still known and called by this name back in Nepal.

The second type of migration had also started in earnest almost at the same time, and they mainly chose the eastern and the western routes, following the step of the conquering Gorkha army. When the Gorkhali Army captured the Kumaon and Garhwal areas in the West of Nepal by 1807, Gorkhali civilians came with them and started settling in those Gorkhali-occupied places there. As a result, Gorkha communities in places like Almora, Nainital, Dehradun, Mussoorie, Simla, Dharmshala, Subathu, Nahan, Balkoh, and Pithoraghad in the northwestern region of India were established almost two centuries ago and are still thriving as of today.

After the Gorkhali army annexed Sikkim, Darjeeling, and the lower parts of Bhutan in the 1780s, the Gorkhali people started moving towards those newly acquired places. But they were forced back to Nepal after the Gorkhali Army lost to the British in the Anglo-Gorkha War 1814-16.

When the British started colonising the northeastern parts of India, they found many empty, inhospitable, uncultivated vast lands. They instantly realised the urgency of a massive workforce to turn the areas liveable if they were to hold on to those newly conquered lands. They needed people living there for security reasons and needed them fast. The British adopted three groups of people to fulfil that particular problem. The first group was the pastoralists and marginal farmers. The British encouraged Gorkhali people from the eastern hills of Nepal to migrate to those barren places with the promise of being allocated the cultivatable lands they managed to create. The Gorkhali came in significant numbers and brought their animals (cows and buffaloes) along. The British wanted the Gorkhalis to settle down in the unused land, such as the forest fringe, the land around the river sites, and the uncultivated land of the tribals for agriculture and animal husbandry. The Gorkhas settled in hills and foothills, cleared the jungles and ravines, cultivated the riverbanks, and created liveable villages through farming and cows grazing in empty and barren lands.

After the Gorkha King captured the Kathmandu valley, the Newari community, renowned for business acumen, felt threatened. Some fled to eastern Nepal, eventually settling down in Darjeeling and Kalimpong. This second group of artisans and semi-skilled professionals would subsequently play a significant part in making the Gorkhali community and its economy in northeast India.

The third group of settlers consisted of the ex-soldiers. With their inborn qualities of industry, perseverance, and military discipline, they turned the newly acquired settlements into a thriving peasantry. Having an army pension also helped improve their daily life. Most of the Gorkhali villages in the remote border areas of the northeast region were formed by them and still make up most of the populations today.

To connect northeast India to the rest of the country, the British had to build more roads, bridges, and railroads, and more Gorkhalis were brought in to work on those projects as labourers. The finding of the new frontiers also provided unique opportunities, and new industries opened up such as mining, logging, and tea plantations, which required a greater workforce. As the population grew, they also needed household servants, security guards, and porters. The solution for all the British's problems came in a readymade package—the Gorkhali people—and the cunning Britishers used them to the fullest.

To protect British Tea Estates and their settlements against the tribal raids, the British created a militia called 'Cachar Levy' in 1835, with two Gorkha companies employed from the very beginning. Headquartered at Cherrapunji, this Force was initially renamed the 'Frontier Force' and carried out punitive expeditions across the borders of Assam. After shifting its headquarters to Shillong in 1864, the Force was reorganised into three Assam Military Police Battalions named Lushai Hills, Lakhimpur, and Naga Hills in 1870. During the Great War, the Assam Military Police sent over 3000 men to Europe and the Middle East, and they fought alongside the Rifle Regiments as a part of the British Army. In recognition of their work, they changed the name of the Force to Assam Rifles in 1917. The Assam Rifles had 46 battalions, a training centre, and several logistics units. Men serving in the Assam Rifles were primarily recruited from Nepal, and the Gorkhali communities from northeastern India; *Khas Kura* is the lingua franca of the regiment. Over 50 per cent of men in the Force are of Nepali origin as of today.

Gorkhalis are mostly hill people accustomed to frugal living, hardships, and a simple life with minimal expectations. Alongside the beltline of the hilly mountains, engulfed between the Himalayas and the northern parts of the Indian subcontinent, extending from Kashmir to the West to the north, Burma is where they feel at home. Despite the struggles, harsh weather conditions, and resentment, millions of Gorkhalis have been living in places like Sikkim, Darjeeling, Kalimpong, Siliguri, Doars, Assam, Meghalaya, Manipur, Mizoram, Nagaland, and Arunachal Pradesh for centuries, and we can still find several thriving communities there even today.

After 200 years, unfortunately, not much has changed for some Gorkhalis, many of whom still rely on cow-herding today. I visited Raid Marwet, a Gorkhali village in Jhorabat Mawsamai, Meghalaya, where each household still relied on their cows for their livelihood, just as they had for five generations. Whenever there were racial and political movements, the Gorkhalis were always the first target. They suffered greatly during times of change such as the Assam movement, the Bodo movement, and the Gorkhaland movement. They were lynched by angry protesters, had their homes and cowsheds burned down, and got uprooted from their villages on many occasions.

Over a hundred thousand Gorkhalis were deported from Bhutan alone and had to resettle in foreign countries as refugees after Bhutan refused to accept them. They suffered from the discrimination of not being able to buy land in those tribal states, having no voting rights, and being forced to abandon the lands they had been renting for thirty years. Despite being there for centuries, born and raised from the ground, Gorkhalis from the Sikkim, Darjeeling, and Kalimpong areas faced racist abuses regularly. They even got told to go back to Nepal.

Since the implementation of the *Treaty of Peace and Friendship of 1950*, the lines between the Indian Domiciled Gorkhalis and Nepali migrant workers have been blurred, all of them unitedly treated as outsiders. This situation has created a grave identity crisis, and the Gorkhalis, who have been living in India as Indian citizens for generations, are not happy at all. It has also created an unwanted rift between the two sides, and one needs to find a solution before it comes to a boiling point.

About 15 million Gorkhalis are estimated to reside in India, and a million Nepalis take up work in India at a time. About 2.6 million Nepali migrant workers can be found spread across the Gulf nations, South Korea, and Malaysia. Countries like Japan, Hong Kong, Australia, New Zealand, the UK, Europe, Canada, and the USA are the main destinations of Nepali youths and professionals, and they do not hesitate to use every way possible, including illegal practices, to get there. Due to many unscrupulous and illegal brokers, Nepali migrant workers have also worked in risky places like Iraq, Afghanistan, and other war-torn countries. Some unlucky ones have paid the ultimate price with their own lives. Stranded in unknown and hostile places with nowhere to go, many have suffered indescribable and long-lasting mental stress. Working under inhumane conditions and extreme heat without proper protection and equipment, constantly subjected to unregulated working hours, many have died and returned home in a wooden box. Nobody notices that the modern and glittering football stadiums in Qatar have been smeared with innocent Nepali workers' blood while they enjoy and celebrate the beautiful game with their rich friends, families, and associates. Nepali workers regularly beaten up and treated like cattle by their masters in the Gulf nations is nothing new, and neither is the plight of those rotting in

Saudi or Malaysian prisons for committing minor religious mistakes. Stories about Nepali workers being used, abused, and exploited by people are heard regularly, yet we seem unable to do anything to stop them.

The practice of '*Muglan Pasne*' (going abroad for a better opportunity) for the Nepalis might have started two centuries ago, but not much has changed even today. With scarce jobs; lack of opportunity; almost zero industry; crippling bureaucracy and corruption; a moribund economy; a society infested with favouritism, nepotism, and cronyism; a country surviving on remittance; and with useless, visionless, spineless, and shameless leaders who would sacrifice anything to remain in power, the chance of being a strong, prosperous, and self-reliant country is the last thing the Nepalis could hope for. As a result, for the country's youths, there are no other options but to jump on the first opportunity to go abroad. No wonder the passport issuing office and the departure gate at the international airport in Kathmandu are always crowded with line after line of departing youths. The young dream about finding ways to shift abroad and private schools and institutions conduct lessons on how to maximise their chances of being qualified for a trip abroad. A connection with foreign people, communities, and institutions is the most sought-after prize for all of the country's young, bright, and talented people. Almost like it's a life-or-death situation for them all, everybody wants to get out. The brain drain problem has become so severe and prevalent that only the old, weak, and helpless, and those who have benefited from this sorry situation, remain in the country.

Despite all this, one thing has never changed in the last two hundred years—the Gorkha grief. The Nepali people started going out of the country for a better opportunity, as they had been two hundred years prior; they are still doing it two hundred years later. Nothing much has changed and they still haven't figure out whose fault is it.

What happened to the Nepali people and the communities? What happened to the country? How did they arrive at such a sorry situation? Whose responsibility is this? Are they to blame themselves? Or has some powerful outside force played a hand in their condition? Why has the country become so dependent? Why does nothing happen without foreign aid or donation money? Are Nepalis that weak and useless?

The irony of our fate can be pretty cruel sometimes, and the truth is always bitter. Instead of selling our skills, expertise, and talent, Nepalis are selling themselves, and selling the most precious assets of a country—the youths. Undeniably, a government that sells its most precious asset cannot expect to be in a good position. Even worse, they have been selling it for the last two hundred years. Hasn't it been log enough?

Nepal has also become a playing field for many outside powers, notably India, China, the USA, the UK, Australia, and other European countries. In other developed countries, foreign embassies and dignitaries have long avoided public engagements, particularly with the media, for the unnecessary risk of being accused of interfering in the host nation's internal affairs. But here in Nepal, they openly engage in almost every event in the country, both in cities and the villages far away from the capital. Kathmandu is full of offices for embassies, INGOs, and foreign-related institutions, and one can always find a person with a connection to them. Their influence is seen almost everywhere. So much so that one could be forgiven for feeling confused about who was running the country, as it seems like nothing happens without their permission. The Nepali government has hopelessly begged for donations for anything and everything, turning the country into beggars.

Still, nobody is asking a critical question—how did we arrive at such a dire, hopeless, and undignified situation?

Until they start asking that vital question and seeking answers, the chance of improving their livelihood, let alone the country, remains zero—the suffering of the Nepali people will continue. Writing about the grief of your people is never easy, and I wish I never had to write about it in the first place. But unfortunately, I have no choice, for nobody will if I do not write about them. The onus is on me, and I am doing my best, hoping that people do not vilify me for writing the truth. I am ready to take all the flak for it, even if they do.

This book tries to seek the right answers and highlight them so the next generation do not have to suffer the same grief that the older generations have for ages; so they can make the right choice eventually, for themselves, for the country, and for good.

The Indian Gorkha Brigade

In the early nineteenth century, Nepal was one of the regional powers in South Asia, along with the British, the Marathas, and the Sikhs. Nepal's borders extended from Kangra Valley in the West (in Himachal Pradesh today) to the Teesta River in the East (in Sikkim today). Since the British and the Gorkhali forces were on an expansion course, they were bound to lock horns sooner or later. They fought a decisive war in 1814, now known as the Anglo-Gorkha War. The war ended after fighting in two phases, resulting in a humiliating defeat for the Gorkhas. The Gorkhas, outgunned and outnumbered, signed the *Sugauli Treaty*, losing almost all their newly acquired lands. With their severely clipped wings, Nepal would never be the same power again. It no longer presented a threat to British rule in India.

But impressed by the Gorkhas' courage, tenacity, and fighting prowess, the British decided to hire them into their army and formed three Gorkha battalions in the middle of the war in 1815. These battalions consisted of about 5000 Gorkha deserters. The British achieved three main goals from the Sugauli Treaty—establishing a British residency in Kathmandu, opening up a trade route to Tibet, and taking the sting out of the loss for the Gorkhali force by enlisting the Gorkhas in the British Indian Army. Enlisting the Gorkhas into the army turned out to be a masterstroke by the British. The Gorkha institution that began in 1815 is still vital today and continues to affect Gorkha lives over 200 years later.

By India's independence in 1947, the British had ten Gorkha Regiments (Eleventh Gorkha Rifles being raised and disbanded after the end of World War I) within their Army. Four (Second, Sixth, Seventh, and Tenth Gorkha Rifles) out of ten Gorkha Regiments followed the British and moved to Malaysia/Singapore in 1948. The remaining six Gorkha Regiments stayed behind and became part of the newly formed Indian National Army. Many Gorkhas from the British side of the regiments refused to go with them; therefore, they had to resurrect the disbanded 11 GR to accommodate them, making the number of the Gorkha Regiments in the Indian Army seven. Since the book is about the Indian Gorkha Brigade, we will only list those seven Indian Gorkha Regiments in the chapter while leaving out the four British Gorkha Regiments.

By the end of the first phase of the Anglo-Gorkha War, the British had already gathered around 5,000 men, mainly irregulars, deserters, and volunteers from the defeated Gorkhali force. After non-Gorkhas were posted to local corps and pioneers within the British Indian forces, three Gorkha battalions were raised in 1815. The Gorkha Regiments (GR), designed as a special crack infantry force, have been leading from the frontline of every major war India had faced under British rule and as an independent country over the last two hundred years and have never failed in its duty.

The Indian Gorkha Brigade have won three Param Vir Chakras (PVC), the highest award for bravery in combat, and hundreds of other battle honours and awards in its distinguished history. They were Captain Gurbachan Singh Salaria, First GR, Congo crisis, 1961; Major Dhan Singh Thapa, Eighth GR, the Sino-India war, 1962; and Captain Manoj Kumar Panday, Eleventh GR, the Kargil war, 1999. The Gorkha Brigade also produced three Army Chiefs, Field Marshal SHFJ Manekshaw Eitghth GR, General Dalbir Singh Suhag Fifth GR, and Chief of Defence Staff General Bipin Rawat Eleventh GR.

First Gorkha Rifles

The First Gorkha Rifles, also known as the Malaun Regiment, was initially formed as part of the East India Company's Bengal Army in 1815 in Subathu (Himachal Pradesh) as the Nasiri battalion and was transferred to the Indian National Army after 1947. As one of the oldest Gorkha Regiments (GR) of the Indian Army, it has a long and distinguished history unparalleled to many other regiments, and it can proudly show its medals and commendations won from different theatres of wars to prove its achievements. The infantry regiment of the Indian National Army is composed of soldiers of Nepali origin, especially martial tribes of Magars and Gurungs from mid-western and western parts of Nepal.

Despite being started as an irregular force, the First GR claimed its first battle honour against the Jats, also known as the *Siege of Bharatpur 1825-28*. Only a little has happened since then, and they spent much of the time chasing dacoits in those wild places. The regiment got involved in a real battle during the first and second Sikh Wars and won two battle honours and a dozen orders of merit. In 1850, the regiment became the 66 Gorkha Regiment of the Bengal Native Infantry. It gained its present numerical designation as the First Gorkha Regiment in 1861, only after it became a part of the force that helped quell the Indian Mutiny of 1857-58 and earned the respect of its colonial master—the British.

The First GR also held the record of being the first regiment that had served outside India when the Regiment under the command of Colonel J. S. Rawlins took part in the effort to quell a rebellion in Malaya during the Perak War in 1876. Fighting broke out after the Malays killed the then-British resident James W.W. Birch, but the rising had already been put down by the time the First GR arrived. The detachment soon fought with the Malays, earning a Victoria Cross (VC) for British Captain G.N. Channer and the Order of Merit (the eligible bravery award for Gorkhas then) for two Gorkhas in honour of their brave actions.

After raising the Second battalion, it became the First Gorkha (Rifles) Regiment in 1891 and went over many changes to the name before becoming the First Gorkha Rifles following India's independence in 1947. The Regiment took part in many operations, such as the third Burma (Myanmar) conflict in 1885, the North-West Frontiers campaigns in the 1890s, at the Waziristan attack 1894, the Tirah campaign in 1897, and the third Afghan war in 1919.

In both First World War 1914-18 and Second World War 1939-45, the First GR was heavily involved and fought in various theatres of war in Europe, the Middle East, Africa, and Asia. During the First World War, the strength of all Gorkha Rifles had increased to five battalions from the two it had earlier, and men from the First GR were deployed to the Western Front in France. They saw actions in defence of Givenchy, the battle of Neuve Chapelle, the second battle of Ypres, the battle of Festubert, and the battle of Loos. After withdrawal from Europe, the First GR fought in Mesopotamia (Western Asia region situated between Tigris and Euphrates river systems) at Kut-al-Amara, Baghdad, Palestine, and the battle of Megido and Sharon against the Ottomans, earning the Regiment a total of eleven battle honours and four theatre honours.

In the Second World War, the First GR primarily saw actions in Malaya and Burma (Myanmar), fighting against the Imperial Japanese Force. After sustaining a heavy loss during the engagement at the Slim River Bridge, the Allied forces had withdrawn to Singapore from Malaya and suffered a humiliating defeat at the hand of the invading Japanese Force. Singapore was eventually felled on 15 February 1942, with 130,000 British, Australian, and Empire troops, including men of the First GR, taken as prisoners by the Japanese.

In Burma (Myanmar), men from the First GR fought in the Arakan campaign and the decisive battle of Imphal and Kohima. The Burma campaign ended after the capture of the capital Rangoon (Yangon) by the Allied Forces on 3 May

1945, paving the way for the end of the Second World War by 2 September 1945.

The first and third battalions of the First GR were deployed in Vietnam to disarm the Japanese forces and help repatriate them back to Japan. But soon they were embroiled in the fight against the Viet Minh to help restore the French control over the country. They left Vietnam right before the start of the First Indo-China War once the French reinforcements arrived. The fourth battalion of the First GR also served in Thailand to disarm the Japanese.

After India's independence in 1947, the Regiment was retained as a part of the newly formed India National Army and became the First Gorkha Rifle in 1950. It currently has six battalions and is stationed at Subathu, Himachal Pradesh.

In the post-independence era, the First GR participated in campaigns such as the Goa Liberation 1961, Jammu and Kashmir 1965 and 1971, Kalidhar 1965, Darsana 1971, and East Pakistan 1971.

The sixth battalion of the First GR was raised on 1 April 2016 at Subathu, the first Gorkha battalion to have come up in fifty years. The ratio between the Nepali Gorkhas and the Indian-resident Gorkhas in the Army's seven regiments had been around 60:40. Being the first Gorkha battalion comprising only of the locally domiciled Gorkhas, the 6/First GR, made history and became known as the Kanchhi Paltan (the youngest one) within the Indian Gorkha Regiments.

Third Gorkha Rifles

The Third Gorkha Rifles was one of the Gorkha original regiments raised in Almora in 1815 at the end of the first phase of the Anglo-Gorkha War 1814-16, and was called the Kumaon Regiment. Initially, the Regiment consisted of mostly men of Kumaon and Garhwali origins and used to police the border with Nepal, earning its first battle honour during the Sepoy Mutiny 1857-58. Before the Regiment gained its present numeral designation, the Third Gorkha (The Kumaon) Regiment, in 1861, it was titled the Eighteenth Bengal Native Infantry of the then Bengal Army.

The Regiment was a part of the march to seize Kandahar in the Second Afghan War 1878-80 and took part in the Third Burmese War in 1885-87. The Regiment, however, was made famous by the storming of the Dargai Heights in 1897, during the Tirah Campaign of the Northwest Frontier and eventually became the Third Gorkha Rifles in 1891.

During the First World War, men from the Third GR served in the Western Front of Europe and saw actions in places like La Bassee, the defence of Festubert, Givenchy, Neuve Chapelle, Aubers, and the battle of Loos. Rifleman Kulbir Thapa of the Second battalion won his Victoria Cross (VC) for performing an unprecedented act of compassion near the village of Fauquissart by saving lives in a highly harsh situation—he became the first Gorkha recipient of the award. He retired in a medical ground as a havildar and passed away at the age of 68 in 1956 in his home village in Nepal.

After Europe, the Regiment fought in Palestine, Mesopotamia, and Sharon against the Ottman Empire. The Second VC of the Regiment came in the battle of El Kefr, Egypt, when Rifleman Karna Bahadur Rana won the award for bravery. With a Lewis gun in his hand, he killed an enemy gunner and captured the gun post, neutralizing the enemy attack by rapidly firing at the enemy's gun post. In 1973, he passed away at 74 at his village in Gulmi, west Nepal.

The Regiment won eighteen battle honours in the First World War. After the end of the First World War, the Regiment took part in the Third Afghan War in 1919 and spent much of its time in the Northwest Frontier and Burma.

In the Second World War, the Third GR served in Italy, North Africa, Malaya, Iraq, Java, Indonesia, and Burma, and won several battle honours for the Regiment. In Italy, the Regiment fought in the battles of Monte Della Gorgace, II

Castello, and Gothic Line in north of Florence, Monte Farneto, and Monte Cavallo. The Regiment also fought the Germans in the battle of Tobruk in Egypt, and many ended up as prisoners.

In Burma, men from the Regiment fought in the battles of Tuitum Ridge, Sittang, Kohima, Imphal, Scraggy Hill, Myitkyina, and Pegu. Honorary Captain Birta Sing Gurung of the 1/Third GR became the only recipient of the Order of the Patriotic War, First Class Russian Red Star among the Gorkhas for leading a successful attack agaisnt the Japanese-held Kangla Tumbi Hill in Burma and neutralised the threat from the Japanese to the Kohima-Manipur ration supply.

In the post-independence era, the Regiment stayed with the Indian National Army and became the Third Gorkha Rifles. The Third GR participated in the battles of Uri, Jammu and Kashmir 1947-48; Shingo River Valley, Kargil 1971; and Nagaland 1956. The Regiment currently stations at Varanasi, Uttar Pradesh, with five battalions. It draws its workforce from the Gurung, Thapa, Magar, and Pun clans from Mid-Western Nepal and the Indian-domiciled Gorkhas.

Fourth Gorkha Rifles

The Nepal Durbar only supported Gorkha's recruitment policy once Prime Minister Jang Bahadur Rana visited the UK in 1850 and saw firsthand the British Empire's wealth and power. He realised the importance of being on good terms with the British and agreed to raise another Gorkha battalion as a goodwill gesture to the British for the sake of their friendship between the two countries. After the first three battalions were introduced in 1815, the Fourth Gorkha battalion was formed in 1857 at Pithoragarh (Uttarakhand) and was initially called the 'Extra Goorkha Regiment'. The Regiment was the nineteenth Regiment of the Bengal Native Infantry before becoming the next Goorkha Regiment in 1861.

Renamed as the Fourth Gorkha (Rifles) Regiment in 1891, they participated in campaigns in India's North-East and North-West Frontiers, the Second Afghan War 1878-80, Waziristan Campaign 1894, and the Tirah Campaign 1897. The Regiment also participated in the Boxer Rebellion in 1900 as part of the expeditionary Force deployed to China.

During the First World War, the Regiment saw actions in the battles of Givenchy, Neuve Chapelle, Ypres, Aubers, Festubert, and Flanders in France. In Mesopotamia (Iraq), soldiers from the Fourth GR fought in Tigris 1916, Kut 1917, Baghdad 1916-18, other battles in Egypt 1916 and in the Gallipoli campaign 1915.

The Regiment also fought in the Third Afghanistan War in 1919 before the Second World War began, in which it saw actions in Iraq, Syria, Cyprus, Egypt, and Italy. In Burma, men from the Regiment fought in the battle of Sittang Bridge, Imphal, Mandalay Hill, Kohima, Bishenpur, and the Arakan Campaign. The 3/Fourth battalion became part of the famous Chindits campaign created by Major General Orde Wingate, renowned for his brilliancy and eccentricity in surgical warfare, which was killed in an air crash during the Second Chindits Operation inside Burma.

After India's independence, it became the Fourth Gorkha Rifles of the Indian National Army and was stationed at Subathu, Himachal Pradesh, with five battalions. Men from the Gurungs and Magars hill tribes of Nepal and Indian Gorkhas make up its central Force.

The Regiment saw actions in the Jammu and Kashmir war 1947-48, the Chinese aggression 1962, Punjab 1965, Jammu and Kashmir 1971, Siachen 1987, and Kargil 1999. The Regiment also served in Lebanon as a part of the UN Peacekeeping Mission in 1998-99 and is considered one of the most highly decorated regiments of the Indian Army.

John Masters, a celebrated British author (*Bugles and a Tiger*, *The Road Past Mandalay*, and more) and a lieutenant colonel, was from the Fourth GR. He once commanded the 3/Fourth GR during the Second Chindits operation in WWII in Burma.

Fifth Gorkha Rifles

After he helped quell the Sepoy Mutiny 1857-58, the relationship between the British in India and Nepal improved significantly. Jang Bahadur offered to form a new Gorkha Regiment to celebrate their new friendship. As a result, a new Gorkha Regiment was formed in 1858 as the Twenty-fifth Native Punjab Infantry, also known as 'The Hazara Goorkha Battalion', and renamed the Fifth Gorkha Regiment in 1861.

Since the Regiment spent most of its earlier time in the Hazara region of North-West Frontiers, it was renamed the Fifth Gorkha Rifles (Frontier Force) in 1903. The first battle the men from the Fifth GR fought outside India was in the Second Afghan war 1878-80 and earned its mettle before the First World War.

In the First World War, men from the Fifth GR served in the Middle East, Gallipoli, and Iraq. Between the First and the Second World Wars, the Regiment fought in the Third Afghan War 1919 and spent most of its time fighting the tribal forces in the North-West Frontiers.

During the Second World War, the Regiment participated in many battlefields, including those in the Mediterranean, Middle East, Italy, and Burma, and won a staggering four VCs during their campaign. Rifleman Thaman Gurung won the VC for bravery in the Monte San Bortolo, Italy battle. He showed tremendous bravery and courage to neutralise the German enemy by firing his Tommy gun and sacrificing his life while providing cover for his troops to move to a safer place. Naik Agamshingh Rai was awarded the VC for his courage in recapturing two critical posts known as 'Water Piquet' and 'Mortar Bluff' in Burma. He also killed three Japanese soldiers on the spot and captured the post. He retired as an honorary captain and passed away in 2000. Havildar Gaje Ghale won the third VC for the Regiment in the battle of Chin Hill, Burma, for bravery when, despite being wounded, he encouraged his men to attack and capture a key position in the fight against the Japanese. He retired as an honorary captain, lived in Almora, India, and passed away in 2000. Subedar Netra Bahadur Thapa posthumously won the fourth VC in the battle of Bishenpur for his ultimate sacrifice.

After the end of the Second World War, the Second Battalion of the Fifth GR was posted to Tokyo, Japan, as a part of the British Commonwealth Occupation force in 1946.

After the independence, the Regiment became a part of the Indian National Army and was renamed the Fifth Gorkha Rifles (Frontier Force) in 1950. In the post-independence era, the Regiment participated in almost all significant actions of the Indian Army and made itself one of the most decorated regiments within the Army. The Indo-Pakistan war of 1947-48, the Hyderabad Liberation of 1948, the Indo-China war of 1962, and the Indo-Pakistan war of 1965 and 1971. The Regiment also participated in Sri Lanka as a part of the Indian Peace Keeping Force in 1987-90 and fought against the Tamil Tigers.

The Fifth GR comprising Gorkha soldiers of both Indian and Nepali origin is currently stationed at Shillong, Meghalaya, with six battalions.

Eighth Gorkha Rifles

The Regiment started as the Sixteenth Sylhet Local Battalion in 1824 as a part of the British East India Company. It went through many transitions before becoming the Eighth Gorkha Rifles in 1907. Known as the 'Shiny Eight' in the Gorkha fraternity of the Indian Army, the Regiment is currently based at Shillong, Meghalaya, with six infantry battalions and a mechanised infantry battalion. The Regiment also produced highly regarded army officers like Field Marshall Sam Manekshaw of the Indian Army, who was affectionately known as 'Sam Bahadur' within his Regiment and was proud of its long and distinguished history.

The Regiment draws its workforce from both Nepal and Indian-domiciled Gorkhas. It is the only Gorkha regiment that manufactured the *khukuri* (the Gorkha knife) during the heat of the Second World War.

The Regiment saw actions in the first Burmese War 1824-25, the Bhutan War 1864-65, and first operational mission against the Nagaland Rebels in 1879, the Manipur Expedition in 1891, and the Younghusband Tibet Expedition 1904.

In the First World War, men from the Regiment fought in several theatres of wars in Europe, the Middle East, and North Africa. They earned fourteen battle honours: La Bassee, Festubert, Givenchy, Neuve Chapelle, Aubers, Flanders, Egypt, Megiddo, Sharon, Palestine, Tigris, Kut, Baghdad and Mesopotamia, to name a few.

In the Second World War, soldiers from the Eighth GR fought in Italy, Iraq, Egypt, Libya, and the Burma campaigns, winning another VC and twenty-two battle honours. At Taungdaw, on the west bank of the Irrawaddy River in Burma, Rifleman Lachhiman Gurung held up an attacking Japanese army for four hours by himself alone. He fired machine guns non-stop, picking up the grenades the enemy had hurled at him and throwing them back, resulting in thirty-one bodies out of the eighty-seven lying killed in front of him, eventually earning him a VC for his magnificent example of bravery and courage. He passed away aged 92 in 2010 in London. The Regiment's battle honours include Iraq, North Africa, Gothic line, Capriano, Gaiana Crossing, Point 551, Bishenpur, Mandalay, Singhu, Sittang, Imphal, and many more.

As one of the six regiments staying with the Indian National Army after 1947, the Regiment was renamed the Eighth Gorkha Rifles. It saw its first action in post-independence India in the Leh operation in 1948. Major Dhan Singh Thapa won the Param Vir Chakra (PVC) in the Sino-India war in 1962. Assumed dead while fighting bravely against the Chinese, he was posthumously awarded the PVC. In reality, he was not killed but lost and unaccounted for during the battle and taken as a prisoner of war by the Chinese. After the war and after being released from the Chinese prison, he returned in 1963, retired as a lieutenant colonel, and passed away in 2005.

The Eighth GR also fought in both Indo-Pakistan wars in 1965 and 1971 and participated in Sri Lanka as a part of the Indian Peace Keeping Force in 1987-90 against the Liberation Tiger of Tamil Eelam (LTTE).

Ninth Gorkha Rifles

Known as the 'Khas Paltan', the Regiment mainly recruits soldiers from the Chhetri (Kshatriya) and Thakuri clans of Nepal and Indian-domiciled Gorkhas. It started as the 'Fatehgarh Levy' in 1817, then it was renamed 'the Sixty-third Regiment of the Bengal Native Infantry in 1823, and eventually changed to 'the Ninth Bengal Native Infantry' in 1857. The Regiment saw its first actions at the Siege of Bharatpur 1825-26, the First Sikh War 1845-46, North-West Frontiers, and the Second Afghan War 1878-80.

The Regiment became a wholly Gorkha unit of Khas origin and was designated the Ninth Gorkha Rifles in 1903. Currently stationed at Varanasi, Uttar Pradesh, the Regiment has five infantry battalions.

In the First World War, the Regiment fought in various battles in Europe and the Middle East, earning several battle honours for the Regiment, such as La Bassee, Festubert, Neuve Chapelle, Armentieres, Givenchy, Aubers, Loos, France and Flanders, Tigris, Kut-al-Amara, and Mesopotamia.

During the Second World War, the Regiment participated in various battlefields across Europe, North Africa, and Burma. The Regiment fought under General Tucker at Fatnassa Heights, Djebel Garci, and Tobruk in North Africa. They also fought in the battles of Cassino I, Hangman's Hill, and San Marino, Italy. In the battle of San Marino, Rifleman Sher Bahadur Thapa received a VC (posthumously) for his display of unparalleled bravery when, despite being wounded in an ambush, he kept on charging at the enemy. Firing his Bren gun, he neutralised the enemy attack and rescued two wounded soldiers but he was killed in the action. Two battalions of the Regiment, the 3/Ninth GR and 4/Ninth GR, formed a part of the famous Chindits in the Burma campaign. The Regiment also saw actions in Malaya, Singapore, and various operations in Burma.

In the post-independence era as the Ninth Gorkha Rifles of the Indian National Army, the Regiment fought a brutal war at Namka Chu, Arunachal Pradesh in 1962; Philora, Punjab in the India-Pakistan war in 1965; and Kumarkhali, Jammu and Kashmir, and Dera Baba Nanak, Punjab in India-Pakistan war 1971.

It was also the soldiers of the Ninth GR who formed a part of the command of Brigadier General Reginald Dyer who fired into the crowd at the Jallianwala Bagh incident in Amritsar, Punjab, on 13 April 1919.

Eleventh Gorkha Rifles

The Eleventh Gorkha Rifles has a unique record of being raised in the middle of the war in the Middle East in May 1918 with four battalions and saw actions in Palestine during the First World War. The Regiment was first deployed at the Suez Canal, Gaza, and the Plain of Sharon in Palestine. After the end of the First World War, the Regiment fought in the Third Afghan war in 1919 and was officially disbanded in 1922.

After India's independence in 1947, the Gorkha regiments of the British Indian Army were divided between the newly formed Indian Army and the British Army. The transfer was on a volunteer basis, and they held a referendum among the soldiers of the four regiments (Second, Sixth, Seventh, and 10th) that would join the British Army. Many men from the Seventh and 10th GR opted to join the Indian Army. Seventh and 10th GR predominantly recruited men from Eastern Nepal, mainly from the Rais, Limbus, and Sunuwars clans, to retain a contingent from this part of Nepal. The Indian Army decided to re-raise the Eleventh Gorkha Rifles on 1 January 1948. Rifleman Ganju Lama, who won the VC in the Second World War for knocking off enemy tanks during the battle of Ningthoukhong, Burma, was originally from the 1/Seventh GR and later joined the Eleventh Gorkha Rifles. He retired as an honorary captain after being appointed president's ADC (aide-de-camp) in 1965. He lived in Sikkim until he died in 2000, and in his honour, several roads, museums, and memorial gates, including the main military base in Gangtok Sikkim, are named after him.

Since then, the Regiment has seen actions in all primary military operations in post-independence India, including the Annexation of Hyderabad in 1948, the India-Pakistan wars of 1948, 1965, and 1971, and the Kargil war of 1999. Captain Manoj K. Panday posthumously received the Param Vir Chakra, India's highest military award, for his bravery and sacrifice in the Kargil war in 1999.

The Regiment has also undertaken two overseas missions to Congo and Lebanon as a part of the United Nation's Peacekeeping Forces.

The Regiment draws its workforce mostly from East Nepal and the Indian-domiciled Gorkhas from Darjeeling and Sikkim. Currently, at Lucknow, Uttar Pradesh, the Regiment has six infantry battalions and a Territorial Army battalion in Darjeeling.

The Recruiting Procedure

Recruiting young men for the Gorkha regiments was a risky task initially, for the Nepal Durbar had not sanctioned it and had deemed it illegal instead, making it punishable by heavy penalties. Those caught in the illegal activity were subjected to harsh treatment, such as being roughly beaten up enough to sustain bodily harm, having property confiscated, and to some extent, even risking being killed. To avoid such ordeals, the Gorkhas were encouraged to settle around the army camps with their families and started a new practice of Gorkha sons following their fathers in training so they could join the Regiment once they became adults.

Once Bir Shumsher officially sanctioned the recruiting policy of Nepali men joining the Gorkha regiments in 1886, no such difficulties persisted, and recruiting practices became much more straightforward. Regiments were solely responsible for finding and training their recruits and were well-equipped with the necessary facilities. The Commanding Officer and the Gorkha Subedar Major appointed the regiment's recruiting agents (known as Gallawalas). Soldiers returning from the extended leave back in Nepal also brought along some men who happened to be most of their friends and relatives from the same village. Alternatively, a group of young men would travel from Nepal to the regimental camps in India and join the Army after going through a general physical test.

It has been over 200 years since the first Gorkha joined the British Indian Army, and the recruiting procedures have significantly improved. As of today, 42,000 Gorkhas are serving in the Indian Army. They have three main pension camps in Kathmandu, Pokhara, and Dharan, and several seasonal centres around Nepal that help distribute pensions for the 125,000 former Gorkhas. The recruiting team from the Indian Army go on a recruiting rally each year, making the selection through those camps before returning to India.

According to the ninety-eight-year-old havildar clerk Dirgha Bahadur Chhetri, who served in 5/Eighth GR from 1944 to 1953 and currently lives in Bhaktapur, there are twenty-eight ex-Army Boards in twenty-eight districts, seasonal offices in twenty-two districts, and a hospital and a medical and welfare centre in Kathmandu, Pokhara, and Dharan. The pensioners receive free medical check-ups and essential medicines regularly in those facilities.

The Indian Army recruits about 2000 men yearly and takes them to Gorakhpur. The recruit training is held in the regiment, but they combine the recruits for two to three units and arrange the training at one of the camps in turns. Due to dwindling recruit numbers in recent years, some of the seasonable camps have been closed down. During the COVID-19 pandemic of 2020-23, no recruiting rallies took place.

The Gorkha pensioners receive free medical benefits through medical cards and old age allowances, and pensions are mainly distributed through direct banking. All these activities are carried out under the watchful eye of the Indian Embassy in Lazimpat, Kathmandu, Nepal.

The ratio between Nepal-domiciled and Indian-domiciled Gorkhas in the Gorkha regiments was 80:20 initially, and then became 60:40. The Indian Army intended to create a 40:60 ratio next, as they wanted more recruits from the Indian-domiciled Gorkhas. For an unknown reason, however, the Indian army has been recruiting less recruits from the Indian-domiciled Gorkhas, and filling the quota by recruiting men from the Garhwal and Kumaon origins. They introduced the 'Agniveer' policy in the Indian Army—a scheme wherein selected candidates will be enrolled for four years. After completing this period, only 25 per cent of Agniveers will be offered an opportunity to apply for enrolment in the permanent cadre. At the same time, the rest will be released to society—which might have grave implications for the Gorkhas in Nepal. Furthermore, the new policy also goes against the Tripartite Treaty of 1947 signed by the three countries (British, India, and Nepal) regarding the Gorkha's enlistment. Expressing its disagreement, the Nepali government halted the recruiting process in Sep 2022 until further notice and asked for dialogue before the recruitment could continue.

As of December 2023, the recruitment of the Gorkhas in the Indian army from Nepal was still suspended, and neither government seemed to be in a hurry to resume dialogue to solve the issue.

The Gorkha recruitment in the Indian Army from Nepal that has been postponed for the last three years has not yet been resumed as I write this page. Despite calls from both sides for dialogue, discussions between Nepal and India have yet to occur, and people are concerned. Due to new changes in the recruitment policy, people are raising questions about the future of the Indian Gorkha Brigade, which can have severe implications for the relations between both countries. While Nepal has asked for a dialogue insisting that the 'Agniveer' policy goes against the Tripartite Treaty of 1947, India does not seem to be in a hurry to solve the stalemate. The over 207-year-old legacy remains at risk but India does not seem like they are panicking, appearing unconcerned as they act as if nothing has happened.

To appease its nationalist egos, India always aspires to rely on the men from the Garhwals, Kumaons, and the Indian-domiciled Gorkhas for the needs of its Gorkha Brigade. The Garhwal and Kumaon people have the same surnames as the Gorkhas and share the same history within the Gorkha Brigade. Most importantly, they will have no problems filling the Gorkha boots if asked for a reason. They have been waiting desperately for this opportunity for years and will not hesitate at all to jump on the first chance they see. They harbour a grudge against the Gorkhas for lording over them in the early nineteen century when the Gorkhas occupied their territories, and they would do anything in their power for an opportunity to return the favour. Taking over the Gorkha's position in the Indian Army would be sweet revenge for the Garhwal and Kumaon communities, and experts have suggested that they have been plotting this for a long time. This might also be why the top army brasses from the Indian side have not seemed worried and are not preparing to start a dialogue with Nepal. It could signify a new beginning for the Gorkha Brigade in India, and the time has come for the people to accept whatever the outcome is for good.

Sharing the Gorkha Veteran's Stories

As my surname suggests, I come from the community at the centre of the Gorkha story and have lived through it to be able to tell it. Places like Gorkha, Lamjung, Tanahu, Kaski, Parbat, Syangja, Baglung, and Palpa of Mid-Western Nepal are the hotbeds of the Gorkha recruitment. Pokhara, also known as the 'Lahure Town', is where most of the former Gorkhas spent their retired lives, making it a permanent base of Gorkha recruitment and a pension centre for both the British and the Indian armies. The Gurung villages in the surrounding areas hardly have a household that has no connection with the Gorkhas. Whether it was their grandfathers, uncles, brothers, or sisters, they have always had somebody who has served or intends to serve the Gorkhas in the future. The Gorkha practice is so ingrained into the community that the youths from the Gurung villages do not think of anything other than joining the Gorkha as their first career choice. I was one of them and became a Gorkha at seventeen and served the British Gorkha for thirteen years before pursuing an alternative career.

Being one of them comes with a few advantages, and easy accessibility to the community is one of them. Despite being uncomfortable talking about my people's grief, bringing their stories to the world is the one job I am proud of, and I couldn't be happier doing it. I had the privilege of talking with many of the ex-Gorkhas, and I am pleased to share their stories with the world.

Eighty-three-year-old Havildar Aiman Gurung from Sikles village, who served with 1/First GR and fought in both India-Pakistan Wars in 1965 and 1971 still remembers the harsh days of the war, when he was hit by a bullet on the helmet and survived on a stale *roti* (flat bread) dropped in the dark by a helicopter. They had to feel for it on the ground as they could not use lights. He had to leave the army abruptly and come home after fifteen years of service. Five members of his family had died all at once, and he had to return to take care of the rest. That unfortunate incident almost drove him insane, he said, but he currently lives happily with his family and works as a farmer in the village.

Eighty-year-old Havildar Major Indra Bahadur Gurung from Lamjung of 4/Third GR said he used a khukuri to fight off the enemy in the India-Pakistan war in 1965, then served in the Indo-Pak war in 1971, and also handled Bangladeshi refugees. Unfortunately, he had a heartbreaking story to tell us. He was unfairly dismissed in 1979 and has been fighting for justice for the last forty years. He had sought help from the Nepal government; approached all the Prime Ministers, embassies, and foreign ministers; and waited in front of the Nepal Embassy in Delhi for nine days. Yet, nothing happened. His long and costly wait for justice continues today.

'As we got deployed at Turtuk airport, Ladakh, in 1972, I was the gun no.1 carrying the sight and the base plate. We moved around until ten or eleven at night, and the fighting suddenly stopped because of the sudden death of King Mahendra of Nepal. After three months, we were replaced, and the war ended with no casualties. It was a newly gained site for India and renamed *The Gorkha Reach*', said seventy-nine-year-old Naik Jagan Singh Gurung of 4/Fourth GR from Gorkha. The most challenging thing he could remember was being deployed in a remote place for three months without proper communication and external connection, with no chance of buying food or clothes, worrying over a depleting food supply.

One-hundred-and-two-year-old WWII veteran, Havildar  Major Chandra Sing Gurung of the 6/Fifth GR, who was from Sikles but currently lives in Pokhara, says he was not afraid of war because he had sworn to fight the enemy and had the blessing of all the Gods and Goddesses from his village. He fought in Italy, Iraq, Iran, and Palestine for five years during the Second World

War, saw many dead people fall during the war, and retired with an NCR 38/month pension in 1961. 'After my one-hundredth birthday, I qualify for an NCR 100,000 monthly pension', he said with a grin. He had two sons: one died in Kashmir, and another, Jit Bahadur Gurung, served in the same regiment as his father, the 6/Fifth GR, and recently retired as a Subedar Major.

Eighty-six-years-old Honorary Captain Tek Bahadur Gurung from Chitwan served with the 5/Eighth GR and fought almost all the major wars in post-independence India, including the Naga Hill Guerilla War 1962, the Sino-India War 1962, the Indo-Pak Wars 1965/1971, and the Mizoram Guerilla War 1976/77. He has a staggering fifteen war medals to prove his valour. 'In the China War, more people died from cold than bullets; they were moved every four hours and avoided getting injured but the Indian Army was not trained in snow, they only started training after the war began, and soldiers were frozen to death in a guarding position', he recalled.

Eighty-four-year-old Naik Ram Bahadur Chhetri from Damauli served in the 3/Ninth GR from 1957 to 1973 and saw actions in both Indo-Pak wars. After losing a leg in a minefield during the 1971 war, he kept crawling forward while bleeding, only stopping when he met a friendly troop. He was carried on a soldier's back for almost a kilometre before he lost consciousness. When he woke up in a hospital in Jalandhar, he cried for a month and begged the doctors to kill him. He saw his leg cut off in a Pune hospital and returned to the regiment with an artificial leg. When he returned home on a four-month leave, he asked for an early discharge. After all those years, he still has to go to Pune every two years to replace the artificial leg and try to get it in Nepal.

'My only grievance as of today is they should have given me at least one bravery medal, but I got nothing', he said with a sad smile. Seeing his smiling face, I instantly knew why he survived all those ordeals—witnessing his positive attitude genuinely humbled me.

'Our main tasks were performing reconnaissance, patrolling the areas, and manning security checks on the road. Suspects were then brought to the camp, interrogated, and handed over to the police if proven guilty. We lost between twenty to twenty-five colleagues and some more were injured within a year of deployment. The main causes of the incident were ambushes, traps, and homemade bombs. When we were losing men and patience, the other ranks suggested using the Khukuri to the higher commanders. Once granted, we started hacking everything in our way in sheer rage. The result? The enemy surrendered, and we returned home.' That was Naik Jog Bahadur Limbu, a sixty-five-year-old from Basantapur, Terathum, who served in the 3/Eleventh GR for twenty-two years, talking about his experiences against the Tamil Tigers in Sri Lanka when deployed there as a part of the Indian Army Peace Keeping Force 1987-90. He also had to carry out the unenviable task of bringing his dead friend's ashes to the family back in the village—he could not get over the grief for weeks.

The Gorkhas in Assam Rifles and other Service Corps

It started as a security force to protect tea estates and their settlements against tribal raids in Assam; it already had two Gorkha companies in 1826 and was called the Cacher Levy. In 1835, the militia force had 750 men. Renamed the Frontier Force, they started protecting the border areas and merged into the Assam Military Police Battalion in 1870. After 3000 men participated in the First World War in Europe and the Middle East alongside the British Army, the force received its name, *The Assam Rifles*, in 1917.

Assam was the central eastern boundary of the British Indian Empire until 1865. The Empire's interest in the area grew as the tea industry developed, and the Assam Rifles initially protected the tea gardens from tribal raids. Encroachments on the tribal areas were made in the name of the trade, and the local tribespeople became suspicious. The British promised to obey the government's orders but they had no intention of keeping their word. The first such operation against the unruly tribespeople was against the Abors. Their offensive expeditions across the border of Assam led the force to reorganize and it was renamed the Frontier Force. The British also issued an army order in 1864 that stated it would be composed chiefly of the Gorkhas and the Assamese Hill-men, with a proportion not exceeding one-fourth of the Hindustanis.

As a part of the paramilitary force, the Assam Rifles assisted in operations against the Nagas and Lushai tribes in the 1870s and the Manipur operation in 1891. The Assam Rifles' main contributions were in opening the region to administration and commerce and they became affectionately known as 'the right arm of the civil and the left arm of the military' in the area.

In the First World War, men from the Assam Rifles fought in various theatres of battle in Europe and the Middle East, earning seventy-six gallantry awards. The name Assam Rifles was assigned in 1917 in recognition of their contribution.

In the Second World War, the Assam Rifles saw actions in Kohima, Sittang River, and Chin Hill, Burma, but the unit had mainly undertaken the task of rear defence closer to home. The Assam Rifles were also tasked with managing and organizing the large influx of refugees who fled from the advancing Japanese Forces into India. The unit won forty-eight bravery awards during the Second World War.

With a strength of only five battalions in 1947, the Assam Rifles, as a part of the North East Frontier Agency (NEFA), functioned under the Ministry of External Affairs since the early years of post-independence India. The Assam Rifles played a crucial role in the rebuilding, resettlement, and rehabilitation of the 1950 Assam Earthquake victims. They were called on to battle in the Sino-Indian War in 1962. Since then, the Assam Rifles have been performing their peacekeeping role in Northeast India in the growing tribal unrest and insurgency, maintaining law and order, and reassuring the people as the primary security force of the region. Additionally, three battalions of the Assam Rifles were deployed in Sri Lanka in 1988-90 as a part of the Indian Peacekeeping Force against the Tamil Tigers.

Admired as 'Friends of the North East People', the Assam Rifles offered a hand of friendship to the region's residents. They were involved in other roles, such as providing medical assistance, overseeing primary education, assisting in reconstruction and agriculture, and handling communications in various remote areas. The Assam Rifles is organised and mandated to perform two tasks—guarding the 1643 kilometres long Indo-Myanmar border as the primary role, and undertaking tasks regarding counter-insurgency as its secondary role. Unlike India's western borders, the Indo-Myanmar border is porous and unfenced along remote and rugged terrains, and manning the border in such a situation is never easy.

The Assam Rifles has grown substantially over the years, and today, it maintains a strong force of approximately 65,000 men with forty-six battalions and various support units and establishments. It was placed under the Ministry of Home Affairs in 1965 for administrative control, and the Army retained operational authority. The Assam Rifles has several headquarters and a training centre that helps train recruits from the army, police, and other disciplinary services. The Assam Rifles also played a vital role in integrating the tribal population into mainstream India.

Headquartered at Shillong, Meghalaya, the Assam Rifles has regional headquarters in the north in Kohima, Nagaland; in the south, in Imphal, Manipur; in the east, in Silchar, Assam; and a training centre and school in Dimapur, Nagaland. In its early days, the Assam Rifles were predominately Gorkhas. Even now, they only make up approximately 40 per cent of the total numbers and mostly come from the local Gorkhali communities in Nepal and India. Khas-Kura, the Gorkhali language, is their unofficial language, and Gorkhali is the predominant culture. From the top hierarchy to the junior leadership, about 80 per cent of the officer cadres of the Assam Rifles come from the Indian Army, and they're responsible for executing the Border Management charter, and Counter Insurgency and Counter Terrorist Operations.

India's long and porous border with Myanmar consists of thick forests, hills, and remote water bodies, scarcely inhabited and extremely inhospitable. The tribal people living in this region are also highly emotional and sensitive. Skills like knowing their language and customs are imperative to fitting in with them and these take years to learn. With decades of experience, the Assam Rifles, are well-established, confident, and live there in harmony, with knowledge of the area familiar to them like the back of their hands. Considering the trust and good relationship they share with the locals, they fit snugly into the job at hand, working to establish themselves as the soul of the region.

On a personal note, I still remember that in my younger days, we had some *Assamko Lahures* (Assamese army men) back in our Gurung village of midwestern Nepal. Since the British and the Indian armies were our main choices, men from other castes such as Bahun, Chhetri, Kaami, and Damai, went to the Assam Rifles, although in insignificant numbers. There was a unique and distinct nature to them that separated them from other *Lahures*—this is the exact reason why I can still recall them. Unlike other *Lahures*, they would come home in their army uniform—a perfectly starched and ironed khaki shirt, short, green canvas shoes with long socks, a Gorkha hat, and an army-issued backpack—and could be quickly spotted from a far distance. They would don the same uniform once their long leave was over and return to join their regiment back in India. That was more than forty-five years ago, and similar scenes are nonexistent in modern-day Nepal.

In addition to the Indian Gorkha Brigade and the Assam Rifles, the Gorkhas also serve in the Jammu and Kashmir Rifles, Garhwal Regiment, and Kumaon Regiment. Ten thousand Gorkhalis serve in other service corps such as aviation, navy, mechanical, medical, supply ordinance, artillery, engineering, and signals in India. The Gorkhas also serve in security forces such as BSF (Border Security Force), CISF (Central Industrial Security Force), CRPF (Central Reserve Police Force), ITBF (Indo-Tibetan Border Police), and SSB (Sashastra Seema Bal). Since there is no provision for recruiting them directly from

Nepal, mainly Indian-domiciled Gorkhas serve in these forces. Those Gorkhas from Nepal must go to India first and find a way to join the forces.

In a nutshell, the Gorkhas play a vital role in the security and defence of a greater India, and everyone should note their contribution.

The Gorkhas in the Garhwal Divsion

When the Gorkhali army captured the Kumaon and Garhwal areas in 1807, Gorkhali civilians soon began settling there. Besides becoming soldiers, they engaged in farming and animal husbandry and worked as security guards, porters, and in manual labour jobs. Joining the British Indian Army was still illegal in Nepal, and authorities used to threaten and beat them, and confiscate everything they possessed as a punishment to deter Gorkhas from doing so. Some were even beaten to death, scaring the hell out of other potential candidates who aspired to join the army in India. To help alleviate their safety concerns, the British encouraged Gorkhas to bring their families with them and settle in the areas near the army camps. In 1864, British India published *The Gorkha Charter*, allowing the Gorkhas to buy lands permanently and settle down in India. Since then, Gorkhali communities have sprouted in places like Bhagsu, Balkoh, Simla, Ranikhet, Nainital, Almora, Dehradun, and many other regions. Uttarakhand and Himachal Pradesh alone probably have a population of about 1.5 million Indian Gorkhas living in the states today.

Before the advent of the First World War, the Dehradun valley and its surrounding areas had already become one of the main army cantonments in northwest India. Everyone living there were, in one way or another, related to the army garrisons. Since the Garhwals and Kumaons came originally from those areas, there was no surprise that they also made up the most numbers in the army. The Gorkhas came along with the establishment of the British Indian Gorkha Brigade. They started residing near the army camps, creating several Gorkhali communities over the years, making Dehradun the biggest one.

The Indian Independence Movement gained momentum during and after the First World War, creating an ever-growing threat to the British and their settlements in India. Offering a resettlement opportunity to the retiring Gorkhas around those key places was another ploy for protecting the British interests in India and a reason behind the Gorkha villages sprouting in those hills and other places in the northwest and east of India.

Rightly so, Dehradun has a special place in Gorkha's history, for the Gorkha saga started right there. It was the Khalanga Fort, a small hill situated on the outskirts of the city area, where Captain Balbhadra Kunwar and his six hundred men, women, and children taught the British troops how a battle should be fought with sheer grit, courage, and tenacity by holding off the superior British force in both numbers and weaponry for almost a month. The British were so impressed by the Gorkha's bravery that they enlisted them in the British Forces in the middle of the battle, starting an institution that would last for over two centuries and one that is still going strong today.

That was also the main reason why I started my research trip to India from Dehradun and it was how I had the opportunity to meet various people from the Gorkha community. After driving through a warren of army barracks, we finally arrived at the Gorkhali Sudhar Sangh (GSS) compound at Garhi Cantt and met Honorary Captain Padam Singh Thapa, the chairperson, to have an hour-long chat over some tea. He talked about the critical roles GSS played in the well-being and the developments of the Gorkha community in Dehradun and listed the excellent works the GSS has done during his tenure. In brief, he said the GSS helped everyone who came to them and always did their utmost best to solve people's problems.

Afterwards, we met the vice chairwoman, Ms Pooja Subba, who visited the library and the main hall. We left the GSS compound after taking a group photograph, realising that GSS was doing an excellent job for the Gorkhas community.

On our way back, the chairperson came to us and told us in a voice tinged with an air of grievance, 'I wished Nepali elites stop talking about Lipulekh; that creates unnecessary troubles for us. Whenever something happens in Nepal against India, it's always us who must bear all the brunt of anger here, you know.' Those were his exact words, which sounded pretty normal to me. After all, they were the ones who had to live there and face it daily, for they didn't have the choice of being able to go to Nepal and stay there until the situation had calmed down.

It started raining as we climbed up a misty hill with tall trees on both sides of the road, and the rain stayed with us until we arrived at the top of the hill. In front of us was a tall gate with black tiled pillars and a red metal panel. A black tile staircase appeared in the middle of a red tile floor, and a red metal pillar with a triangle base was erected on the top of the stairs. Three Khukuris and a spear facing upward the sky were attached on the top as the crown of the pillar, and a surrounding wall protected the whole area. 'Thank you for visiting the historical memorial—Khalanga War Memorial' were the words inscribed in red letters on the top of the entrance.

Before I became emotional, we returned to the car and headed down the hill the same way we had come up. It took some time to find our next destination—the Khalanga Monument—at Shastradhara Road. The rain had already stopped when we finally arrived. As we entered the site, two white marble inscriptions stood on both sides of the pathway, on which descriptions of the Gorkhas' bravery in the Khalanga fort was inscribed. With collonaded green plants, colourful flowers, and green lawns on both sides, we walked on the red tiles and reached the centre. The centrepiece of the monument, the famous two white obelisks built in honour of the two army commanders in the Khalanga/Nalapaani fort during the Anglo-Gorkha War 1814-16, Major General Rollo Gillespie and Captain Balbhadra Kunwor, stood proudly, surrounded by greenery, separated by an inner wall and a green gate. Next to it stood a dried tree, and a black crow sat on it. It is likely one of the rarest monuments, where the winning side, the British, had built a memorial in tribute to a commander from the losing side, and it has become one of the top tourist attractions in Dehradun for years.

Captain Balbhadra Kunwar of Nalapani fame is a widely known national hero in Nepal. He is commonly read in school textbooks, and every Nepali child knows about him. After the Nalapani war, he joined the Sikh Khalsa Army of Punjab's Maharaja Ranjit Singh and died in the last battle. While in Kathmandu, I had the privilege of visiting his ancestral land in Balkot, which he received from the Nepal Durbar in return for his contribution to the country. According to Krishna and Shusma Kunwar, the sixth generation of Balbhadra Kunwar, their ancestral land covered an entire hill and slopes of its surrounding areas in the early days. Some of his cousins were still living in the area. Most of land was sold now, and only the ancestral temple and its surrounding grounds remained as a remnant of its past glory. Given their situation, all I could do was wish them all the best.

The next day, we met Ms Madhu Gurung, an author and the director of the radio Gham Chhaya, and her staff Col Jeevan Chhetri, Bhupendra Adhikari, and the team. We also had an opportunity to participate in one of the programs for Radio Gham Chhaya, the Gorkhali Community FM Radio serving the 1.5 million Gorkhas in Northwest India for good.

We also had the privilege of meeting up with Lt General (Retd) Shakti Gurung PVSM, UYSM, AVSM, VSM, one of the two highest-ranking military officers from the Gorkha community—the other being Lt General (Retd) R.S. Pradhan—and listened to his views on the achievements and challenges facing by the Gorkha community today. It was from him I heard about the general classifications among citizens in India for the very first time. The General Caste (GC), Scheduled Tribe (ST), Scheduled Caste (SC), Other Backward Castes (OBC) where the Gorkhas were classified, and the newly added Economically Weaker Caste (EWC)— governmental jobs, positions, and resources in India are allocated according to this classification.

According to General Gurung, a bulk of the Gorkhas in Uttarakhand are from the uniformed services. Having served in the defence services and paramilitary forces, the men who retired and came home did not care much about what happened outside their home compound. 'Surya Asth Gorkha Mast' is the standard joke that goes around here, which means the moment the sun goes down, a Gorkha opens his bottle, and that's the end of all his cares in the world. He also expressed concerns about the community's lack of unity, the ignorance of Gorkha culture and traditions, and about the identity. Landmarks related to the Gorkha community of the past are slowly dying or are being subsumed by the local environment. For instance, the Gorkha Military Inter College (GMIC), raised by the British in 1925 and situated on military land, was a prized school at one time and can be aptly termed as a heritage school of Dehradun. It had close to 4,000 students in the 1960s but has only 143 students today. *Dashain* is still celebrated with enthusiasm and excitement, and so is *Teej* by the ladies, though—he concluded.

We also learned about many Gorkhas from Dehradun, who fought for India's independence as freedom fighters against the British during the Second World War. They came mainly from the 2/First, 2/Second, and 2/Ninth Gorkha Rifles, which served as a part of the Allied Forces against the Japanese in Southeast Asia and suffered a humiliating defeat in Malaysia before the infamous British Singapore fall on 15 February 1942. Taken as prisoners of war (POW) by the Japanese in Singapore, it was here that Captain Mohan Singh of the Indian Native Corps raised the first INA (Indian National Army), and many of the Gorkhas from Dehradun joined the Army of the Free-India Campaign. Freedom Fighters like Tej Bahadur Thapa, Tej Bahadur Subba, Dal Bahadur Thapa, Durba Singh Thapa, Bir Singh Khatri, Bir Bahadur Gurung, Bishan Singh Rana, Ram Singh Gurung, Hira Singh Khatri, and many more had sacrificed for the independence and duly remembered by the Gorkha community.

Among them stood Khadka Bahadur Singh Bista, who saved a young woman from the hellish confinement of a wealthy lord by wounding him with a blunt khukuri. Known to the community as the 'Rajkumari Kanda' (The Princess Incident), he is revered by the Gorkha community. Another well-known freedom fighter from the community was Major Puran Singh Thakur (Khawas), who played a significant role in establishing the first batch of the INA in Singapore and served a prison term after being captured in the battle of Imphal and Kohima. He was also heavily involved during the anti-Rana regime 1948-50 in Nepal and commanded the Freedom Fighters against the Ranas, serving as the Inspector General of Police (IGP) in Nepal in the 1950s.

The famous one among them was Durga Malla, who fought for India's independence against the British armies in the Second World War as an intelligent officer of the INA (the Indian National Army) under Netaji Subhash Chandra Bose. Deployed in Malaysia with one of the Gorkha battalions, he joined the INA raised by Captain Mohan Singh, was involved with drawing recruits to the INA, and entered India through Burma as an intelligent officer (Major) of the INA. Captured in Ukhrul, Manipur and taken to the Red Fort and made to stand in the INA trial, he was given a few chances to accept that he was wrong to join the INA. Even his wife was brought before him, and still, he wouldn't budge. He was sentenced to death on 15 August and hanged at Delhi's Central Jail on 25 August 1944. Durga Malla is remembered as a martyr on 'Balidan Diwas' (Martyr's Day), observed by India's Gorkha communities every year. A statue dedicated to him was erected on the parliament grounds in Delhi in 2004. A similar figure of Durga Malla was also erected at Garidhura village, Darjeeling.

We briefly met with some community writers on our last day in Dehradun and discussed writing. Before leaving Dehradun, thanks to Col (Retd) Jeevan Chhetri, we visited the Lal (Red) Gate, formerly known as the 'Second Goorkhas Memorial Arch of the Second King Edwards VII's Own Gorkha Rifles' inside one of the army barracks, which was built just before the WW1 in memory of all those fallen men from the regiment in its 100-year-old history. After going through the list of familiar surnames such as Gurung, Magar, Thapa, and so on for some time, we left Dehradun and headed towards Nainital, our next destination.

Dehradun was home to many Gorkha regiments before 1947. In post-independence India, it has accommodated chiefly the Garhwals, Kumaons, and other units. The Indian Military Academy (IMA), established in 1932 and involved in training officers for the Indian Army, is the crown jewel of an army city like Dehradun.

We arrived at Nainital late at night and stayed in a hotel with a Nepali guy as our caretaker. It was where words of a famous army song, *'Nainital, Naini Tal, Ghumi Aayo Rail, Ankhama Laune Kaalo Gazal Bulbulema Tel, Naini Tal'* originated and could still be heard today in the army barracks during special functions. As an army veteran, I still remember singing the song during our training days in 1980 in Hong Kong, and it was my main reason for wanting to visit the place first. The beauty of the hilly mountainous town called Nainital appeared in front of us only the following day, when we got up early and ventured out. As we walked along the side of Lake Nainital, enjoying the fantastic views of the hotels and lodges on the opposite of the hill, we wondered how they managed to pile up house after house on top of each other. I realised why the British sent the tired, war-trodden and injured Gorkhas here to recuperate after they had returned from WW1 and WW2. Initially, a small number of Gorkha regiments used to have their base here and in Almora. The area where the Gorkhas had resided before was occupied by a three-story building when we visited. An Army Rest and Recoup Centre located at the front side of the lake also confirmed its legacy as a place where tired and injured soldiers go went heal. Although our visit to this beautiful healing place was brief, it was enough for us to learn about its importance in Gorkha's legacy. We left the area knowing that all the efforts we had put into coming here was well-spent.

Another group of Gorkhas who are less well-known and visible than their army cousins also dwell persistently in these parts of India for work. They are known as migrant workers from the Far-Western hills of Nepal, such as Kalikot, Dailekh, Humla, Jumla, Darchula, Doti, Baitadi, Bajura, Bajhang, Dadeldura and the surroundings. Migrants from Surkhet go to Simla, Kullu, Ladakh, and Indian Punjab. Places like Pithoragarh, Almora, Nainital, Ranikhet, Kedarnath, Haridwar, Rishikesh, Dehradun, and Mussoorie are the obvious choice of destinations for the Nepali migrant workers, for they provide work in a similar environment, weather, and terrain as they have back at home. They work as labourers on the roads and porters in the marketplaces. Despite playing an essential role in the functioning of those prosperous cities, they mostly end up doing other lowly paid odd jobs, putting themselves at risk of being used and exploited.

Nepal's far-western region is remote, underdeveloped, and downtrodden, with primarily high hills and rugged terrains. Far away from the powerbrokers of Kathmandu, it has hardly seen any developments in decades, consigning people there to a harsh and challenging life for generations. The only option the people here have is to crossover to the Indian border, toil as a labourer or porter, come home with a meagre saving for a brief rest and restart the whole process again year after year until their bodies give up. Security guards, porters, labourers, delivery boys, waiters, construction workers, house servants, drivers, caretakers, seasonal workers in the fields, street cleaners, and many more lowly paid manual jobs are what they do in India and earn the least within the community.

The irony of this pathetic situation is that such lousy jobs are considered a lot better than the situation back home. If they had a better option, nobody would have troubled coming here. Fate can be cruel, but as the reality bites in, they will have no choice but to toil on, and unfortunately, that's the reality here.

As we drove around the Gorkhali community in Dehradun, we didn't see any signs that alluded to Nepali people living there. They neither dressed, nor walked, nor talked like Nepalis. There were no Nepali-typed tea stall, nor small community gatherings, nor a shouting match over trivial issues between neighbours over the balcony. To me, it was an Indian neighbourhood, and that was it. Had I not met so many Nepalis inside the GSS compound, I would have never believed they lived in that same neighbourhood. They have become so immersed in the mainstream community that they have become one of them and found acceptance and protection within the community. That may be for the best in the end. After living with the mainstream communities for generations, the Gorkhali community must have learned the bitter lesson—one needs to become part of the mainstream culture and get acceptance if one is to live in peace and develop as a community. Especially to a minority, it's a matter of survival, and for the Gorkhali community here in Dehradun, and other parts of India, things were no different.

Through work, intermarriage, and adaptation, the Gorkhali community has assimilated well with the locals, including the Garhwals and Kumaons. I am sure they will carry on doing what needs to be done, and the good people of Dehradun and other parts of northwest India will thrive as a proud Gorkhali community, just as they have for the last two hundred years.

The Gorkhas in Sikkim, Darjeeling, Kalimpong, and Bhutan

The Lepchas and Bhutias, the two prominent communities from Sikkim, were also known as 'the sons of the soil' in the region. They originally came down from Tibet and became 'Blood-borthers' after signing the Blood Treaty at Kabi Lungchuk and started settling down in the lands in the fourteenth century. When the Gorkhali Army annexed Sikkim in 1779, the Gorkhali people also started settling down in the same area. The Limbu and Magar tribes were said to have been living there even before the Lepchas and Bhutias arrived from Tibet. Once the Gorkhas lost to the British in the Anglo-Gorkha War 1814-16, the Chogyal (Monarch of Sikkim) and the British signed the Titaliya Treaty in February 1817, which guaranteed Sikkim's security by the British and returned the lands the Gorkha had annexed from Sikkim earlier. In return, the British were given trading rights in Sikkim and passage to the Tibetan Frontier.

The indigenous populations, such as the Lhopos, Mons, Tsongs, Rongs, Lachenpas, Lachungpas, Hapopas, and Bhotias, became 'Sikkimese citizens' or 'Denjongpas' in the Lhopo language, which also meant 'tribal peoples of the Himalayas'. The first elections in Sikkim was held in 1953 based on six seats for the Bhotias-Lepchas and six for the Gorkhas. Due to internal political factions and several appeals to India for help by the king himself and other political parties, Sikkim was incorporated into the state of India in 1975. Today, Sikkim has 340,000 Gorkhas, making up almost 63 per cent of its total population.

There are fantastic tales of how the Gorkhas crossed the mighty Teesta River when there were no bridges to cross to the other side of the river. Legend has it that the Gorkhas gathered at the upper part of the River in winter when the water was low. A strong man would swim across the river with a rope tied to his waist. They tied the rope to trees on both sides of the river, used a big round *nanglo* (a flat round-shaped bamboo basket), placed the children and women on the *nanglo*, and pulled them to safety over the other side of the river. Once everyone had crossed the river, the men untied the rope and swam over to the other side. That is how the Gorkhas reached the other side of the Teesta River for the first time and settled across Sikkim from 1802 to 1809.

Captain George Llyod leased Darjeeling from the Chogyal of Sikkim in 1835. Over time, he turned the hills into a resort for sheltering and recuperating from the sweltering heat of India's plains. There were only a few villages or residences on those hills before the British transformed them into tourist destinations. In 1841, Dr Campbell brought tea plants from Kumaon and started growing them in Beechwood, Darjeeling. Ten thousand men from Nepal migrated in one lot to work in the tea industry as tea pickers, guards, cleaners, porters, servants, etc. Magar, Tamang, Rai, Limbu, Sherpa men and those from other tribes came with their families to work in the tea plantations. Due to their military backgrounds, Gurungs were hired as the Sardar (Group leader) in the tea plantation. Tamangs were said to be forced out of Nepal by Hindus because of their cow-eating habit, and other castes such as the Brahmin, Chhetri, and Newar also migrated subsequently and settled down here as farmers and traders.

Darjeeling is well-known within the British Gorkhas, for almost all of the regimental clerks serving them hailed from

Darjeeling. Among them was eighty-five-year-old Major Jai Angdembe Limbu, a Darjeeling resident, who joined the Boy Company of the Brigade of Gorkhas in 1953, participated in the Malay Emergency 1948-60, the Brunei Revolt 1962, and the Borneo Confrontation 1963-66, and retired after thirty-two years of service as the head clerk at the headquarters of the Brigade of Gorkhas in Hong Kong in 1985. He was also an excellent marathon runner with twenty-six years of experience and a distinguished career full of international full marathons credentials from around Asia. He is currently living in Darjeeling with his wife.

The city of Darjeeling has evolved significantly from where it once started. Kalimpong and Duars were added to Darjeeling only after the Duars War 1864-65, also known as the Anglo-Bhutan War, through the Treaty of Sinchula signed in 1965. After the fall of Kathmandu valley to the Gorkha King in 1767, the Newars, the native of the valley and Nepal's enterprising people, headed eastward and settled down in Kalimpong. After Younghusband's Tibet Expedition of 1903-04 and the discovery of Chumbi valley as the nearest trade route to Tibet, Kalimpong flourished and attracted more people to come and try their luck there. Gorkhas were the only outsiders permitted to carry on trading activities within Tibet, and many from Kathmandu did move there.

After the Duars War, Bhutan ceded about 20 per cent of its southern territories to the British, including the Assam Duars and Bengal Duars, in return for an annual subsidy of 50,000 Rupees. To transform these barren and inhospitable lands into tea gardens and farmland, the British brought in the Gorkhas from Nepal in significant numbers and have been residing there since then. Before the Bhutanese Refugee Crisis in1990s, the Gorkhali made up 34 per cent of Bhutan's total population. After implementing its new policy—One country, one religion, one race, and one language—the entire Gorkha population has come down to about 20 per cent.

By the end of the First World War, India's independence movement had intensified and posed a severe threat to the well-being and properties of British officials living in Darjeeling, Kalimpong, and other parts of India. The Gorkhas were well-known for their bravery, loyalty and discipline, and the British encouraged them to resettle in India after retirement permanently. Only 3900 out of the 11,000 men who were discharged after the First World War returned home in 1919. Many found jobs in India as security guards, servants, drivers, or household servants around those British settlements.

Today, the Gorkhali community makes up almost all of the Darjeeling district's two million population and the area is considered one of the best tourist destinations in India.

Unlike in northwest India, we found Gorkhali-speaking people around us when we crossed the Kakarvitta, Nepal-India border. Whether a taxi driver, a money exchanger, or a shopkeeper, they were all Gorkhalis, our people, and we didn't feel like we were in India. We eventually found a friendly taxi and headed to Salbari, Siliguri.

In Siliguri, we met a group of intellectuals, community leaders, and a community of Ex-Gorkha members. 'In India, we are all Gorkhali (Nepalis), but in Nepal, there are Bahun, Chhetri, Newar, Magar, Gurung, Tamang, Rai, Limbu, Sherpa, Kami, Damai, and many more. That's the difference,' said the intellectuals. The community leaders summarized, 'We are done because of the three Ts—Timber, Tourism, and Tea. If we hadn't had them, the West Bengal government would have served Gorkhaland to us on a platter.' I was moved by the welcoming event arranged by the ex-Gorkhas community at Khoprail, Siliguri. I met some senior Gorkha veterans over tea and heard about their faith in the brave Gorkhas tradition and undying dedication.

We also met Suresh Pradhan in Siliguri, a multi-talented Gorkha veteran who served with the 5/Eighth GR and a living proof that Gorkhas are not only good at soldiering. He is a well-known figure in the community who wears many hats, such as a writer, a social worker, a football team owner, and a community leader. He dedicates his life to the Gorkha community. He is always busy helping people and is known for his benevolent and untiring spirit. Currently, he is busy establishing the Gorkha Charitable Hospital for the Gorkha community in Siliguri, West Bengal.

Climbing up the curvy hills on our way to Darjeeling made me anxious, but it wasn't because of the rough and steep ride. Visiting Darjeeling had always been my wish, for I have known many people from Darjeeling since my army days and heard so much about it. Above them was the Darjeeling Himalayan Railway, built by the British in 1879-81 (together) was an 88-kilometre long route between New Jalpaiguri and Darjeeling, and ascended to a height of 100 metres to 2200 metres along the journey. To my delight, when the rail appeared, both quite loud and majestic, everybody stopped, including us, and let it pass.

The Gorkha War Memorial at Batase Hill was the first stop we had called for, and we noticed all of the visitors there were from India's plains. The centre of the memorial had a tall pillar, a Gorkha soldier with a rifle bowing in front of the post, and circled by a line of granite boards with names of the fallen Gorkhas inscribed on them. Later, I was amazed when I saw the night crowd at Chaurasta and the famous Oxford Bookstore, where I found my book and signed the remaining five copies as requested by the manager.

In Darjeeling, I first noticed how crowded and steep the place was; they had built houses literally on top of each other. Yet, they were accessible by a motorway, which was quite an achievement. Coincidentally, the GTA (Gorkhaland Territorial Administration) election had just taken place, and a new party, Bharatiya Gorkha Prajatantrik Morch (The Indian Gorkha Democratic Front), had just been sworn in. 'We are here to rectify all of our past mistakes. The past parties were too destructive to our cause, and we will do our best to fulfil the wish and aspiration of the hills', promised one of the top leaders of the new ruling party with whom we had a brief conversation.

Interestingly, the Maple lodge we stayed in was a property that once belonged to Nepali Rana PM Jang Bahadur, where one of his sons lived for his schooling in Darjeeling. They had proudly displayed the historical poster as proof in the lobby.

Many hill people also contributed during the free India movement and are fondly remembered by the community. Among them, Gaga Tshering, Jangabir Sapkota (Gandhi Baaje), Tej Bahadur Subba, Narbir Lama, Pratiman Singh Lama, Putalimaya Devi Podhar, Bhakta Bahadur Pradhan, Bhagat Bir Tamang, and Savitri Devi (Helen Lepcha) were some notable names who fought against the British rule and whose legacies live on with the people.

Thinking back, the highlight of our visit to Darjeeling has to be the meeting with Mr Hemant Pradhan, a seventy-year-old man who has dedicated the last fifty years of his life to collecting everything about the Gorkhas and has transformed his home into a private museum. Every inch of his house was filled with items such as army uniforms, badges, equipment, statues, weapons, swords, helmets, war medals, insignias, khukuris, photographs, and many other forms of memorabilia, and his collections had been so vast that it could have put actual museums to shame. Neglected for decades by the community and the relevant authority, he kept working on his mission and used money from his pocket to reach this position. 'I couldn't serve the Army, but I always wanted to do something for the Gorkhas to educate our new generations. My entire life has been dedicated to this project, and my mission has been completed', he told me with a proud and beaming face for which I had nothing but total respect. Fifty years of unwavering dedication is not a small thing, for one must have love, passion, courage, and belief to make it a reality, and he has proven these qualities to the world.

One piece of good news he had for us at the end made us all genuinely happy for him. He has found a permanent home for this collection through a trust called Gorkha War Museum Trust since 2012, and the building was finally ready. He needed some more time to wrap up the internal decorations, but he should soon be done with his passion project. What this man has done for the Gorkhas is unbelievable, and we hope he receives all the support and encouragement from the authority and people.

'My father's (A WW2 veteran, Subedar Ram Chandra Pradhan RIASC) five war medals are the most precious ones among all the collections here', he replied with pride when I enquired, and I instantly knew how he had made his father proud.

On our way to Gangtok, Sikkim, I got slightly emotional as we crossed the Teesta River—the historical river we had heard about since childhood. As Gangtok was a protected area, travelers had to get a special permit—A Protect Area Permit (PAP) for foreigners and an Inner Line Permit (ILP) for Indian citizens—from the police station at Rangpo. Gangtok wasn't a big city, but it was cleaner and tidier than other cities in India. They built the city alongside the main road with small roads joining it on both sides like arteries, ascending from the river valley to high up the hill. Since we had arrived earlier, we managed to visit the famous Mahatma Gandhi Road, Enchey Monastery, and the surrounding areas.

After meeting with a group of intellectuals at the Rachna Book House and an ex-MLA (Member of the Legislative Assembly) at his residence, we learned some interesting facts about the Gorkhas in Sikkim. Among them was a Gorkha whose family owned a factory in Mangpu that processed liquid extracted from the Cinchona tree and used it as tonic water. The drink-loving British in India drank it as a Gin and Tonic until they could import the real thing from the UK, and it became a household drink all over India. The practice dried up after the discovery of synthetic, and Cinchona is currently used mainly for medicinal purposes. Agricultural products such as elaichi (cardamom), orange, and tea, as well as the tourism industry are the backbone of Sikkim's economy, and people mostly rely on governmental jobs.

'As the majority in Sikkim, the natives always come up with a new policy that helps keep us, the Gorkhas, in the minority, and due to lack of unity among us, we are struggling to overcome this pressing problem', the veteran politician explained.

On our way out of Gangtok, I was disappointed about not being able to take a picture in front of the gate of VC winner Ganju Lama Army barracks, for the soldiers guarding the compound politely didn't allow our request. My slight disappointment was sufficiently compensated as I travelled with an old friend from Gangtok to Rangpo on our way to Kalimpong and had time to catch up.

We experienced multiple power outages in the Kalimpong hotel, which reminded me of a chronic problem back in Nepal, where load-shedding was the norm of the day. In the early morning, I walked around the streets and went up to a hill but couldn't make much out of it, for everything was closed, and not many people were around. Kalimpong is known as the centre of writers, thinkers, artisans, and musicians, and our meeting set up with a group of intellectuals was not surprising. 'Due to lack of an ideal visionary and a charismatic leader, we have been suffering as a second-class citizens for decades, and the national identity crisis is our main struggle for us the Gorkhalis', they summarised the central issue of the Indian domiciled Nepalis that even outsiders like us were well aware of. After a brief but lively meeting, we got into the car and headed down to New Jalpaiguri to catch our night train to Guwahati, Assam—our next destination.

★★★

The Gorkhas in the Northeast

Our night train journey from Jalpaiguri to Guwahati Assam was fascinating, for it was my first-ever train ride in India. First, it was more relaxed and unruly than we had imagined thanks to the Bollywood movies, and those people selling food, beverages, and other snacks were more moderate. Under the veil of utter darkness, the train quietly moved ahead, and since there was nothing much to do nor anything to look at outside, we tried to get some sleep. Sleep was the last thing I found; I waited anxiously until the train pulled up at the Kamakhya Railway Station, Guwahati, Assam—our final destination.

The first British military campaign against the Kingdom of Assam was on the Brahmaputra River, as they explored the river on boats fitted with guns. The first intervention came in 1792 when Captain James Welsh from the Madras Army of the British East India Company came to Goalpara in support of the fugitive Ahom King, Gaurinath Singh, and finally managed to settle him to his throne in 1794. The British didn't annex Assam until 1826. By then, the Burmese had already attacked the Assam Kingdom three times and brought it under their control. Rattled by the Burmese aggressiveness, the British had no choice but to take action against the aggressor and fought three consecutive wars with the Burmese. The first Anglo-Burma War started on 5 March

1824 and ended on 24 February 1826, and it helped chase the Burmese out of Assam. The British captured the lower parts of Burma, including the capital Rangoon (Now Yangon), in the second war between 1852-1853, and the British annexed Burma (Now Myanmar) on 1 January 1886 after taking the upper parts of the country in the third war in 1885. During the British occupation, a substantial number of Gorkhali people came to Burma as soldiers, animal rearers, guards, mine workers, porters, servants, gardeners, and labourers, leaving a vibrant community of over 300,000 people as of today in various parts of the country.

After taking control of Assam with the Yandabo Agreement and the notheast region in 1826, the British embarked on a survey and restructuring mission throughout the region. But they found the area replete with warrens of vast forests and barren lands sparsely occupied by tribal people. To clear those forests, marshes, and ravines and make them liveable, they needed a labour force with solid hands, unending persistence, and a willingness to live a frugal life and ask for nothing in return. They also needed labourers for their newly-founded tea industry. The British found a readymade solution to their pressing problem in the shape of Nepali migrants, and all they needed was to ask, albeit with a little encouragement, and as the saying goes, the rest is history.

The first direct contact the Gorkhas had with the region was when they became a part of the Cuttack Legion in 1871. They went on to be known as the Assam Light Infantry, and participated in various operations against the tribal people throughout the region. The next was the economic migrants. The northern hilly and mountainous belt suited the Gorkhas' lifestyle for centuries. It had the same terrain, weather, and resources that they had been familiar with, and migrating to India's northeast region was just an extension of their ongoing pursuit for a better life. As a result, they were okay with moving there and came in significant numbers.

Northeast India, also affectionately known as 'The Seven Sisters States' (Assam, Meghalaya, Manipur, Nagaland, Mizoram, Tripura, and Arunachal Pradesh) of India, have had a strong connection with the Gorkhali people over the last two centuries and the Gorkhas played a significant role in making the region one of the top tourist destinations in India. The northeastern parts of India were primarily jungles and barren lands, and they needed a hard labour force to clear those fields before they could use them for farming. It was also the frontier of the British Empire in India, and it was required to have communal people for security reasons. People of Nepali origin had already started crossing the borders for a better life and heading towards the northeast India after the Anglo-Gorkha War of 1814-16. The British brought them in big numbers as they were good at turning harsh and inhabitable land into cultivatable farms by clearing jungles, shrubs, weeds, and the marshy lands alongside the Brahmaputra River.

Historians have classified Nepali migrants into three categories. First, the pastoralists and marginal farmers. The Gorkhalis were natural herders and managed their animals well. The new lands offered those people, also known as 'Gwalas' (the cow herdsmen), an abundance of grazing grounds for their animals. They came in significant numbers, cleared the forest and ravines and slopes, and created habitable farmlands for animals and men. A score of small and new Gorkhali communities sprouted out in those areas, and initially, they were involved primarily in agriculture, logging, and dairy farming. The hardworking Gorkhalis were well-adapted to such environments. They helped transform the landscape of the whole region by turning most of the inhospitable lands into a terrace of paddy fields and arable lands. The tribal communities of the hills preferred their nomadic type of lifestyle, changing their places according to the practice of Jhum cultivation (also known as the slash-and-burn method of clearing a vegetative or forest cover on a hill or a slope by burning and using the ashes as the potash to the soil) and availability of water. The Gorkhalis stayed within the peripheries longer enough to earn the respect of the locals, and the locals were happy to lease the tribal lands to the Gorkhalis on a crop-sharing basis.

Equipped with an ever-cheerful face, perseverant and firm hand, and carrying his only weapon, the Khukuri, the marginal Gorkhas were ready to do anything to make a living. When the British started constructing motorways, the Gorkhas were there, and the Gorkhas willingly lent their hands of labour when the Railway Company brought trains to the region. When the British found oil at Digboi and other minerals in the area, the Gorkhas happily worked in those mining fields too. The Gorkhas also played a role in the making of the region's tea industry, which the British founded in 1823, and transformed Assam into one of the world's most famous tea gardens as of today.

The second category of Nepali migrants were the ex-soldier settlers. The British had encouraged the resettlement of the retired Gorkhas in India from the very beginning. They did so in this region for two main reasons. Firstly, the tribal people of the area were not only unruly but also vengeful, and they had carried out deadly revenge attacks on the authority. The British administrative premises and their settlements needed protection from such attacks and having loyal, trusted, and disciplined ex-soldiers around them made them safe. Secondly, due to their new and ever-changing assignments, troops were to move their base every two-three years, entailing massive logistic work and exerting a heavy toll, especially on women and children. The burden of having to move around with women and children also affected the soldiers' morale, for they were always worried about the safety and uncertainty of their families. To have peace of mind and be able to do their job correctly, they needed a safer place for their wives and children. Having a permanent base for the regiment and a separate family quarter for the wives and the children next to it was the solution they came up with for good. As a result, the Gorkhas, including the retired ones, were encouraged to resettle in the army camp, creating new cantonments in various parts of the region. The settlement of Manipur, with discharged soldiers right after the end of the First World War, was a testament to the ongoing British policy. Over time, the army camp closed down, and the cantonments remained as Gorkha villages scattered around the region.

In 1867, when Captain Kalu Gurung from the Assam Light Infantry arrived in Shillong, he was said to have described the place as empty, lacking a single rat let alone people. This was how scarcely populated those places were back then.

Going back to the third category of Nepali migrants, we had the artisans and semi-skilled professionals. They came from a feudal caste society in Nepal where their trade of occupation, such as smiths, carpenters, tailors, and traders were determined by their birth. After the discovery of the Chumbi Valley, Sikkim, the trade between Nepal and Tibet almost dried up, and traders and artisans associated with minting gold and silver migrated to Sikkim, Kalimpong and Assam. Since they were employed part-time, full-time, occasionally and seasonally, they floated around the cities and fulfilled the requirements of the un-skilled local communities. Demands for such semi-skilled workers grew as new developments caught up with time, and they started working in various fields other than what they had been doing from birth. They worked as plumbers, masons, mechanics, drivers, electricians, construction workers, security guards, gardeners, bus conductors, cleaners, and in many other roles. They mostly held several roles at once, making themselves available any time of the day and night. Despite being an integral part of the community, they remained invisible, quietly doing their job and earning a simple living for their families.

The Gorkhas migrated to the Northeast and fell roughly into three classes based on occupation. First, the Khutiwalas or the cow herders were mainly Brahmins and some Chhetris. They also brought their wives and families along with them. Second, the daily labourers or the coolies were mainly Damais and Kamis and a few were Rais, Magars, and Gurungs. Third, the men recruited for the Gorkha battalions were from the castes of Gurung, Magar, Rai, and Limbu.

All in all, of roughly every ten Gorkha migrants, two were Brahmin or Chhetri, three Damai or Kami, and five were Magar, Rai, Limbu, and Gurung. Later, the Assamese middle-class Hindu community is also said to have significantly encouraged other Gorkha's migration to Assam. They needed cheap labours to work for them on their newly acquired land and saw the opportunity. The first social institution established in Shillong was the Gorkha Panchayat, which had two categories. One for civilians and another for the cantonment covered by their respective areas. The two merged and became the Gorkha Public Panchayat in 1950. Later, more Gorkha associations were formed, such as the Ex-servicemen Union, the Student Union, and other academic and religious organisations.

The Gorkhali communities mostly settled down on the outskirt of cities and towns to sell milk and dairy products to the urban folks. One can still find Gorkhali villages today in most of the region's seven states, but most are in Assam. The Assam Rifles started with thirty-eight sites, such as Sadiya in Assam, Mokachuk in Nagaland, Aizwal in Mizoram, and Mantripokhari in Manipur. The Gorkhali initially settled in the grazing area such as Burachapari and Tezpur of Chapari area and then in Kaziranga of Golaghat Assam. The other places where the Gorkhas settled were Sonitpur, Tinsukia, NC Hills, Karbi Anglong, Dhemaji, Kokrajhar, Darang, North Lakhimpur, and Kamrup. After the district headquarters shifted from Cherrapunji to Shillong in 1867, they built a Gorkha village in 1891 on land leased from the Syiem of Mylliem, and more Gorkha settlers followed. Places like Pasighat, Changlang, and Itanagar in Arunachal Pradesh; Sadar Hill, Santolabari, Setikhola, Amaledara, and around Imphal areas in Manipur; Bhalukurung, Songpijaang, and Bausedara in Mizoram; Durgabari, Gorkha Basti, and Agartala in Tripura; Barapathar, Mawprem, and Shillong in Meghalaya; Dimapur and Kohima areas in Nagaland; and almost every part of Assam, we have the Gorkhali communities living there. Approximately 2.5 to 3 million Gorkhas call the northeast region of India their home and living there for generations.

Members of the Gorkha communities from the northeast region contributed to the free India movement before 1947, and some even went to jail. Chandra K. Sharma, Nityanand Timsina, Bishnulal Upadhya, Hari Prashad Upadhya, and many more fought against British rule in India and are remembered by history.

After we arrived at Guwahati, Assam, the first place we wanted to visit was the Paltan Bazaar, which was the first Gorkha settlement in Guwahati. The Gorkhali community used to walk, talk, and buy their groceries and household necessities as people usually do from their neighbourhood market. When we arrived there, however, the last thing it resembled was a Gorkhali market; we couldn't even see a vestige of its past existence. With crowded and unclean streets, misplaced shops and eateries, and noisy and unregulated traffic, it looked the same as any other city in India.

Moreover, we could hardly find a Gorkhali face that looked like ours. It was only when we finally arrived at the Hindu Temple and talked with the person at the counter in the Dharmasala (hostel), did we learn that Gorkhalis actually lived in the city. We were in the same area as the old Paltan Bazaar used to be. Within walking distance from the Hindu temple, they had the Gorkha Bhawan, the Headquarter of the Gorkha organisations in Guwahati, where all the community's problems, such as D (doubtful) voters, National Registration of citizenship, land issues, and other issues are solved. Rich, powerful, and successful people, including Gorkhali literary big names like Lil Bahadur Chhetri and many others, were members, and the organisation proudly represented 2.5 million Gorkhas from Assam.

Alongside the main highway after Jhorabat, especially between the Eight Mile and Eleven Mile road where the main highway represents a border between the two states (Assam and Meghalaya), we saw some Gorkhali villages with their typical two-storied tin-houses and the familiar cowsheds scattered on the slopes on both sides of the highway. A distinctive structure stood in the middle of the village and we could hardly miss the familiar Hindu temple easily found in Nepal.

Among these villages was the Raid Marwat Village, Mawsamai, Jhorabat on the Meghalaya side, a village with no more than twenty houses, extended from the roadside to the upper part of a small hill. Barring just a few small shops selling groceries and miscellaneous items, the rest of the houses (one-story houses with straw roofs) on both sides of the road had a cowshed in the background. We had the privilege of talking to one of them—fifty-nine-year-old Gopal Bhujel, a fifth generation cow-herder living there with his family and twenty-six cows.

According to Gopal Bhujel, there exists a union of cow herders like him in Assam, which promotes, protects, and safeguards the industry; they entirely rely on the cows for their livelihood. Since tribal states like Manipur, Mizoram, Meghalaya, Nagaland, and Arunachal Pradesh don't allow outsiders like the Gorkhalis to buy land, cow-herders like Gopal Bhujel lease the land from the tribal people, and the lease usually lasts for thirty years. But they have had no problems extending the lease and living peacefully in the village for the last thirty-five years.

When the outside world caught up with the region and urbanisation rolled on, the Gorkhalis moved out of the city and town areas and resettled at the fringes of jungle, slopes, and hills. Today, one can find remote villages of such kind at the borders with Myanmar in Arunachal Pradesh and other northeast states. Non-tribal people cannot buy lands in Tribal states like Manipur, Mizoram, Meghalaya, Nagaland, and Arunachal Pradesh, nor can new generations transfer their grandparent's land to their grandchildren. They all have to sell the lands to the tribal and only to tribal women; as a result, no Gorkhali can own the land.

According to the tribal tradition, men work at home, and women run the household. Properties are transferred from mother to daughter, and the youngest daughter holds everything. As a result, the Gorkahli communities have to lease the lands from the tribal communities. If they fail to renew the lease, the Gorkhali communities must move to a new place and find new land, creating a new resettlement every thirty-five years. This is why the Gorkhali communities are always on the move and pushing themselves further away to the border areas in search of a new place.

Intermarriage between the tribal and Gorkhali communities is quite common, and they have been living together as neighbours for generations now. In tribal states like Arunachal Pradesh, Mizoram, Nagaland, and Meghalaya, the Gorkhas have no landownership right. They also cannot vote for the members of the Indian lower and upper house. The Gorkhas cultivate tribal lands in a Bhagi (sharing) system and share the crops with their landlords, creating a master-tenant relationship that has served them well over the last two hundred years. The Gorkhas are always careful not to offend their landlords for fear of being kicked out anytime if their landlords are displeased. Gorkha's beautiful daughters are forced to marry tribal men, and the Gorkhas visit their landlord's home during Dashain for blessing. Intermarriage is encouraged, and the Gorkhas also speak tribal language. Children of Gorkha fathers born out of intermarriage take their tribal mother's surnames and seldom mention their fathers in public. It's also normal for the tribal leaders to monitor and discourage the Gorkha's interactions with outsiders. If they find out, the Gorkhas risk the chance of being evicted from their lands. The Gorkhas do what they must do for a living, and the Gorkha's life in the Northeast tribal states has not changed much over the last two hundred years. And yet, they don't utter a word of complaint and quietly carry on with their daily life.

Despite being a citizen of a country for over 200 years, the Gorkhas are still barred from such fundamental rights as owning lands or voting, and the position of both state and central governments is somewhat ambiguous and thus pathetic. It's pretty baffling that such draconian and anarchic rules still do exist in India, and no one has done anything to change that. Although the Gorkhas must share some blame for this issue, the relevant authorities should have been held accountable years ago. It it had not been for the Gorkhas, the tribals in Northeast India would have still been pursuing animal hunting, Jhum (shifting) cultivation, and chasing wild elephants. The Gorkhas had played a significant role in making the region what it is today, and the state should be grateful. The Gorkhas cannot live on as second-class citizens in their own country, and that's much more than gross negligence, if not a crime, on the government's part. To prevent unfair treatment and discrimination, the Gorkhas must change their way of life (mainly migrating, farming, and animal husbandry) to a new one that guarantees their position in the community. The Gorkhas must change their way of living to survive or be consigned to oblivion forever.

We spoke to one of the intellectuals we met at Devkota Nagar, Assam, whose family had started as a cow-herder and had more than five hundred cows at that time. Devkota Nagar was a thick jungle, with roaming tigers days and nights—he reminisced. Assamese, Gorkhali, Hindi, Gaaro, Khasi, and English were the primary teaching languages in the local schools. The Gorkhas are involved in intermarriage with the

Khasi and Gaaro tribes and vice versa. The Gorkha's new generations are getting educated and finding new jobs in industries other than farming and animal husbandry. He also suggested we visit the famous Kamakhya Temple, but due to our early night train, we said goodbye and headed to the train station.

When our night train finally rolled ahead towards our next destination, Jalpaiguri, I was plagued by one particular thought I couldn't get out of my head. The Gorkhali people first came here as cow-herder. Two hundred years later, why are people like Gopal Bhujel still cow herders? Two hundred years is a very long time, and it saddened me that not much has changed in those years. What were all those troubles for? I have so many questions that have no answers, and I firmly believe these innocent people deserve a lot more than they have now.

The Gorkhas in New Delhi and other Parts of India

Over a million Gorkhalis have been working in India at a time and primarily assembled in major cities like New Delhi, Kolkata, Mumbai, Lucknow, Patna, Benaras, and many more. Although the existence of the Gorkhali community was determined by the army base initially, the main factor in recent days has been the migrant workers, who have been moving from one city to another and creating a new Gorkhali community, big or small, in various parts of India.

Benaras has a long and distinguished connection with the Gorkhali communities, a history that stretches back to when even Nepal wasn't formed as a nation. Benaras, has been the home away from home to all political exiles, deposed kings and queens, and individuals who had problems with the Nepali rulers. Since Benaras had all the top schools, children of the Nepali elites and political leaders studied here. Renowned for its top religious (Both Hinduism and Buddhism) universities in India, students of both religions from Nepal came here regularly in significant numbers. Before the centre of power moved to New Delhi, Benaras was the hotbed of Nepali politics, from where they plotted periodically for and against the regime back in Nepal.

Furthermore, everything used and read on paper within Nepal was all printed here, for Nepal had no printing machine or facility by then. Devotees from Nepal also regularly visited

Benaras, one of India's holiest places. On a different note, Benaras was also where Nepali elites hid their illicit fortunes. Some Rana families owned famous, historical, and expensive properties in Benaras.

For only one reason, India has always been the breeding ground for Nepali political parties, including Nepali Congress, Maoists, and others. Almost all Nepali politicians had their education and political aspirations started here in India. They also learned all the political trades to become a successful politician here from Indian politicians, making it unsurprising that they all had close affiliation with Indian politicians in one way or another. They all had regional offices in India before venturing into Nepal, making India a testing ground for all political parties when they were banned in Nepal. Having played such a significant role in the making of Nepali politics, one shouldn't be surprised at all about India being accused of micromanaging Nepal.

Delhi alone is said to have about 2-300,000 Gorkhalis living there. Unlike the old times when they were primarily watchmen, servants, and porters, the new timers are now students, business people, and migrant workers. Political people jockeying for power and position have separate societies and mostly remain detached from the other Gorkhali communities. Laxmi Nagar is mainly for students, and a substantial Gorkhali community is also found in places like Paharganj and Rohini. Those working in lowly odd jobs mostly lived in groups of four to six people and prefer to live discreetly. They come from the same village or area and live and work communally together for a matter of convenience. Bonded by the same origins, they travel and go home together and look after each other. When its necessary, they send money, a parcel, or a message back home when their friends return without them. They find safety in numbers, which is why migrants from Doti and Accham districts go to Mumbai, people from the Bajhang district to Bengaluru, and people from the Bajura district move to Delhi.

Another megacity with a substantial number of Gorkhali communities is Mumbai, home to about 300,000 Gorkhalis. Bollywood might be the first word that crosses people's minds whenever they hear 'Mumbai', and it wouldn't be surprising if some of the Gorkhas also arrived with the same aspiration and dream. But they say that they began travelling to Mumbai due to their military connection before 1935, and they flourished into a vibrant community over time. The community has evolved and its members are engaged in various respectable professions nowadays. To guide, promote, and safeguard the Gorkhali communities, they came together to form an umbrella organisation like 'The United Nepali Organization' in Mumbai and have done their best to protect their interests. To encourage marriages within the community, they even provide a matrimonial site and issue marriage certificates through the organisation.

Before the British shifted India's Capital to Delhi in 1911, Kolkata was the centre of power in India. A substantial number of Gorkhali people, mostly politically affiliated, used to reside there. The political community also shifted to Delhi with the change of power base, leaving mainly the everyday folks behind. Still, about 10,000 Gorkhalis currently live and work in various sectors in Kolkata. Similarly, most cities like Kanpur, Bhopal, Patna, Lucknow, Gorakhpur, Bengaluru, Chennai, Goa, Pune, Nagpur, Ahmedabad, Amritsar, and many more have several Gorkhali communities and its members are its members are seen in various parts of the cities. A pocket of Gorkhali communities is found mainly in Utter Pradesh (UP) and Bihar, the two bordering states of Nepal's south, and the volatile war-torn region of Jammu and Kashmir. Even a remote place like the Jap Gorkha Community in Doranda, Ranchi, Jharkhand, is another example of how the Gorkha communities have established themselves around India and thrived on their own.

Movement trends seem to have formed among migrant

workers as people from certain parts of Nepal tend to go to a particular part of India for good. It may be easier to go to a place where you have friends or relatives already there. Researchers have found that people in the far-western hill district of Achham mostly go to Mumbai and the rest to Bhopal and Indur. Gorkhas from Baitadi join the Indian Army. Those from Bajhang go to Bengaluru, people from Bajura to Delhi, and people from Doti go to Mumbai and Gujarat. All in all, over sixty per cent of the male from Nepal's western hilly districts go to India for work. They also travel in groups for safety reasons and return home before Dashain and Tihar—Nepal's two main festivals.

Apart from becoming soldiers, education, work, medication, and pilgrimage are other factors that bring the Gorkhas here from Nepal. Due to the lack of high-class hospitals and medical facilities in Nepal, most illnesses cannot be treated in Nepal, and one has to come to India for further treatment. The Char Dham (famous for four pilgrimage sites) for the Hindus is in India—Badrinath, Kedarnath, Gangotri, and Yamunotri—attracting millions of Hindu pilgrims from Nepal yearly. Similarly, for Buddhists, Bodhgaya is the must-visit site where Lord Buddha found enlightenment, and devotees from various parts of Nepal flock here regularly.

The types of work Gorkhali migrants do in India are more or less the same, and the patterns repeat itself throughout India. Young boys work in restaurants and Dhabas (roadside eateries); illiterate ones work at the factory, or as a domestic helper, driver, chowkidar, ayah (nursemaid), and porter; and a few lucky ones make it to the low-level clerk, cashier, receptionist, and hawaldar in the Indian police. In short, they are almost everywhere and even share a joke among themselves about this reality—Nepali and potatoes are found everywhere. They mostly work in menial and relatively low-paid jobs, and degrading conditions often involve considerable personal danger, such as physical violence and infection with STDs and HIV/AIDS.

Since Nepal is a poor, underdeveloped, and landlocked country that has three sides covered by India and the north side blocked by the Himalayas, life is hard, and if not India, where else can they go then? Whether it's for education, religious and spiritual needs, healthcare and medication, or in search of a better life, they have no choice but to come down to India, which is why so many Gorkhali people live and work in in India. It's not a matter of choice but an act of survival. Besides, they are not here to beg or scavenge. They are instead here to work, shed sweat, and toil as hard as a poor donkey. And people should at least respect them just for that very reason.

Unfortunately, this phenomenon also has a dark side under the veil of the glamour, attraction, and opportunity offered by the big cities—a heinous act of Gorkhali women being sold and forced to work as sex workers in brothels. Mumbai alone is said to have about 40-45,000, Kolkata has 40,000, and many other big cities around India have ten of thousands each; about 5-7,000 young Gorkhali women are said to be trafficked into India each year. It's a shame that the relevant authorities haven't done much to stop this inhumane and repulsive act of human greed and exploitation. This has to stop, perpetrators must be punished, and all must strongly condemn it.

Vying for Autonomy—The Gorkhaland Movement

When the British leased the hill of Darjeeling from Sikkim in 1835, it was a barren hill with just a few households. Ten thousand Gorkhas from the east of Nepal were brought in to work in the newly found tea plantation; the rest is history. Before 1861 and from 1870-1874, the Darjeeling district was a 'non-regulated area' where acts and regulations of the British Raj did not automatically apply in the district in line with the rest of the country. The status changed to 'a 'scheduled district' in 1874 and to a 'backward tract' by 1919. Darjeeling was known as a 'partially excluded area' from 1935 to 1947, just before India's independence.

The word 'Gorkhaland' is said to have been coined by William Brook Northey in his 1936 book *The Land of the Gorkhas*, which suggested that a large number of Gorkha community lived in Darjeeling may be termed as Indian Gorkhaland.

The ongoing Gorkhaland Movement that is demanding a separate state for the Gorkhalis of Darjeeling, Kalimpong, and Duars from the plains within India's constitution is nothing new. The first voice started with the Morley-Minto reform in 1907 when the Hillman's Association of Darjeeling submitted a memorandum demanding a separate administrative setup. The same group also submitted another memorandum in

1917 to the chief secretary of the Bengal government, the secretary of state of India and the Viceroy for a creation of a separate administrative unit comprising Darjeeling and Jalpaiguri districts. The Hill Association again raised the same demand before the Simon Commission in 1929. A joint petition with Gorkha Officers Association and the Kurseong Gorkha Library was submitted to the secretary of India for separation from Bengal.

The Hillmen's Association tried again in 1941 and asked for the exclusion of Darjeeling from the Bengal province. In April 1947, the Undivided Communist Party of India submitted a memorandum to the Constituent Assembly and Pandit Nehru and Liaquat Ali Khan, demanding the formation of 'Gorkhasthan' comprising Darjeeling, Sikkim, and Nepal. Before the formation of the States Reorganisation Commission (SRC) in 1953, the All India Gorkha League had met the then Prime Minister Nehru in Kalimpong and submitted a memorandum demanding separation from Bengal in 1952. Similarly, the President of District Shramik Sangh also submitted a memorandum to the SRC demanding the formation of a new state comprising Darjeeling, Jalpaiguri and Cooch Behar districts. The All India Gorkha League tried again for an autonomous region in 1954, 1957, 1967, and 1968 but failed.

The situation was so complicated that Darjeeling was reportedly in Pakistan from 14 to 18 August 1947 and a Pakistani flag fluttered over the Darjeeling Town Hall for a full five days.

In return for its contribution of 250,000 Gorkhas to the British cause during the Second World War, Lord Mountbatten, the last Viceroy of India, is said to have forwarded a proposal to Nepal Durbar, offering the return of those territories Nepal had lost after signing the Sugauli Treaty in 1816. Nepal arranged a special meeting with the representatives from both Darjeeling and Dehradun. While a representative from Darjeeling was for it, Dehradun ruled against the idea of joining for a greater Nepal. The Rana regime, advised by the Brahmin Pandits, decided against letting Darjeeling join in for a single reason— The Rana regime saw the academic community of Darjeeling as trouble makers and bringing them inside the home would be like inviting troubles for themselves. As a result, Darjeeling didn't become an integral part of Nepal and has struggled to establish itself since then.

The first shock to the Gorkha's aspiration of a new state came in 1951 when the West Bengal government-orchestrated-census reported only 88958 Gorkhalis in Darjeeling, representing 19.96 per cent of the total population. They counted only Gorkhali-speaking people of Brahmin and Chhetri tribes to distort the reality. Ten years later, in the next census, it was 94 per cent. Darjeeling and Jalpaiguri districts were officially included in West Bengal in 1955 through a bill titled 'Absorbed Area Act 1954' and have remained so today. All the preceding political parties, such as Akhil Bharatiya Gorkha League and so on had tried their best, but it all fell on deaf ears.

After the India-Pakistan wars of 1965 and 1971, Bangladeshi refugees inundated Siliguri and the plains and changed the entire demography of the area. The Bengalis also owned all the businesses and other institutions. By the 1970s, most British-built institutes and industries deteriorated, including the tea gardens. Deforestation became a serious concern, natural herbals and cinchona diminished, and the Darjeeling hills had little to offer by then. It was so dismal so that educated youths had to cross over to Nepal for a livelihood, and many had joined the British Gorkhas as clerks.

Experiencing historical neglect, exploitation, deprivation, and systematic alienation under successive administrations for over a century fuelled their demand for a separate state of Gorkhaland within the constitution of India. It all boiled down to more discontent and alienation among the people.

Tapping on the public's anger gave them the perfect chance for a new agitation. All they needed was someone to step in and lead the way. It was then that the GNLF (Gorkha National Liberation Front) came in and started a violent campaign. GNLF, spearheaded by a writer-turned-political leader, Subash Ghisingh, demanded a separate state from West Bengal consisting of Darjeeling, Kalimpong, Kurseong, and Siliguri. It started with peaceful protests but soon turned into violent agitation, setting government properties on fire during 1986-88, killing 1200 people (unofficial figure said to be way higher) before ending in 1988.

The movement had several grievances, such as the mistreatment of the Indian Gorkhas by the Indo-Nepal Treaty of 1950; the false representation of the Gorkhas population in Darjeeling by the West Bengal government; unfair treatment of the state government during civil unrests in northeast India; the lack of recognition of the Gorkhali language by the Indian constitution; the demand for only the Indian Gorkhas being allowed to enlist in the Indian Army; the deteriorating situation of the tea, timber, and tourism industries in Darjeeling due to the state government's negligence; and lack of recognition of the Gorkha's contributions during the independence movement.

During the two violent years, the hills turned into a battleground, with night raids by the security forces. Men suspected of being a member of the GVC (Gorkha Volunteer Cell) had to hide in the forest to avoid capture and the subsequent brutal beating. Continuous bandhs (closing down shops, transportation and other businesses) and dharnas(sitting-in in front of governmental offices) brought the livelihood of ordinary folks to a standstill. Battles between the Gorkha Revolutionaries and the state government troops were fought almost every night, and the news of government properties being burned down was broadcasted every day. Graffiti of revolutionary slogans appeared on every wall of the city, and a dark cloud of uncertainty hovered over the hills. The government forces' merciless killing of thirteen innocents and injuring another fifty people on 27 July 1986 in Kalimpong was the turning point of the movement, and people have remembered it yearly as 'The Martyr Day' or 'Black Sunday' since then. Burning down ordinary people's houses and properties became the norm of the day, and atrocities committed against innocent people in a revenge attack were prevalent. In one such revenge attack in 1987, they burned down more than 125 houses at Mane Bhanjang and Sukhia Pokhari, and people were shot randomly. After the crackdown on the GNLF leader's house that killed his aide, a forty-day civil strike was called in February 1988, causing schools, shops, and people's livelihoods to come to a screeching halt and eventually costing more than seventy lives on both sides and over five hundred people being arrested.

The movement halted in 1988 after GNLF, West Bengal, and the Union Government signed a tripartite accord known as the Darjeeling Gorkha Hill Council (DGHC). Peace finally descended in Darjeeling after the signing. The arrested were released and came home. The two years of intense struggle ended, and everyone celebrated.

After the first election held on 13 December 1988 for DGHC, GNLF won all seats, and Subash Ghisingh became the Chairman. GNLF went on to rule the hills for the next twenty-one years, but its tenure was riddled with controversies from the very beginning.

The people felt betrayed when the GNLF agreed to drop the demand for a separate state of Gorkhaland. While most of the intellectuals remained silent, the rest aligned with the Chairman to benefit from the newly acquired fruits. In the inclusion of the Nepali language into the Eighth schedule of the Constitution of India in 1992, the Gorkhas found another reason to celebrate. With DGHC, they lost Gorkhaland, and now they got the Nepali language, not Gorkhali. Within a few years of rule, the DGHC had become a hotbed of corruption. Contractors and conspirators forgot people's dream and aspiration of having a separate state; identity along the process. The Chairman morphed into an undisputed supreme leader surrounded by a coterie of greedy and corrupted yes-men and acted like a new emperor.

Internal distrust, frustration, and discontent among the people prompted a brazen attack on Ghisingh that brought the whole hills to a standstill. The army was put on high alert and declared a curfew. A power struggle within the GNLF was the cause of the direct attack on him, and a few more lives had to be sacrificed before he could assert his authority again. To regain his lost ground, Ghisingh found a new tool for religion, directed people to renounce religious practices related to Hinduism, Buddhism, and Christianity, and started worshipping nature and stones to prove themselves as tribal. Another mistake he had committed was trying to internationalise the movement by writing to the Nepali King, Bhutan, and the U.N., which angered New Delhi and led to him being labeled as a secessionist. This was enough to garner enough support against him.

His political suicide came in the form of 'The Sixth Schedule' between 2005-2007, when he suggested, and eventually accepted, the inclusion of DGHC under the Sixth Schedule of the Indian Constitution, which shrank DGHC just to an autonomous tribal area of West Bengal. Members of his party, GNLF, accused him of betrayal and confined him to a resort in Siliguri for three weeks before he eventually resigned. After his resignation, he confined himself to his home in Jalpaiguri until he died in 2015. They also banned him from entering Darjeeling and allowed his body to enter only after his death.

Out of GNLF, a splinter party emerged with Gorkha Janmukti Morcha (GJMM) in 2007, led by Bimal Gurung, Ghisingh's protégé. It reignited the demand for a separate state of Gorkhaland comprising the Darjeeling district, the Duars of Jalpaiguri, and the Alipurduar districts. GNLF continued ruling without Ghisingh for the next four years until the Gorkhaland Territorial Administration (GTA) accord was signed in 2011. No signs of a permanent solution for the Gorkhaland issue appeared on the horizon, and Darjeeling saw two more violent protests in 2013 and 2017. When West Bengal's government decided to impose the Bengali language in all the schools from class one to class ten in 2017, the agitation flared off with GNLF, GJMM, and other political rivals in the hills coming together to demand the Gorkhaland.

The simmering agitation ended only after closing down schools, shops, and tea gardens; burning government offices and vehicles; interrupting the Internet service for twenty-eight; vandalising public properties, hydropower, and railway stations; and allowing seven innocent people to lose their lives. The agitation lasted for 104 days, forcing leaders from GJMM, including the head, Bimal Gurung, into hiding. Even the newly formed GJMM had a splinter from within and colluded with the state government. The breakaway faction called GJMM2, led by Binoy Tamang, governed the GTA under a 'caretaker arrangement' until the next election. The election was won by a new political outfit, called 'The Indian Gorkhas Democratic Front,' and led by Anit Thapa, who took over the GTA's administrative responsibility on 15 July 2022.

Women's contributions to the Gorkhaland movement were never inferior to men's in any respect. Although their roles during the Gorkhaland movement went unnoticed under the leadership of GNLF, women's participation in the hill politics increased after 2007, and the formation of Gorkha Jana Mukti Nari Morcha (GJMNM) led by Dhan Maya Tamang marked a new beginning. After six years of its formation, almost every household in Darjeeling hills had at least one woman as a member of GJMNM and they played a significant role in making the movement successful in its post-2007 phase. They organised and participated in many actions, such as rallies, hunger strikes, picketing, and other civil disobedience activities. 'Doers Chalo Andolan' in 2009 (go to Doers rally) was one of the main ones where women participated in significant numbers, including youths and students. Rallies from the Railway station to Chowk Bazaar of Darjeeling town were a regular feature in those days. Later in 2011, in Sibchu, Doers, the police mercilessly opened fire at the rally and killed two woman activists. To secure justice for the two killed by the police, they declared 10 February 2011 as 'Black Flag Day' and called for more rallies. Despite not being duly credited and appreciated by men, the women of the Darjeeling hills have heavily contributed to the movement. Failing to acknowledge their contributions here would be a grave injustice to them and a wrong step for the community. History has to be fair to them.

Although the Gorkhas' demand for a separate state within the Indian constitution has been going on for over a century, why hasn't the goal been achieved yet? What went wrong? Was the demand itself not strong enough or were there outside factors that hindered them from reaching the ultimate goal? Why did they fail? What were the weaknesses? Was it self-inflicted or due to outside influence? There are so many questions that need answers. It's about time they all stop for a moment, look back, think things over, and try to analyse the situation. They need to take a hard look at themselves and their past mistakes, separate the wrongs from rights, and find the best way to offer them the best chance of delivering their ultimate goal. After all, if India can have twenty-eight states and eight union territories today from the twelve states we had in 1947, why can't it have one more in the name of the Gorkhaland? Maybe the problem comes from the within—the Gorkhas themselves?

We don't have to go through the pages of history to realise the importance of the Gorkhas' contributions to the making of modern India, and I have no intention whatsoever of insulting people's wisdom by repeating the Gorkha history in detail. However, it's imperative to narrate them, at least in brief, to make the point here. After joining the British Indian Army in 1815, there wasn't a single war in which the Gorkha didn't fight. To name a few, the Gorkhas fought the Jats, the Marathas, the Sikhs, the Burmese, the Afghans, and the Tribes from both the northwest to the northeast frontiers so that it could serve a mighty country like present-day India on a platter. Not to mention the crucial part the Gorkhas played during the partition, the free India movement, fighting the state's enemy in wars and protecting the borders in post-independence India. The Gorkhas did all the fighting for the country, so the rest could sleep and work in peace.

The crucial part the Indian-domiciled Gorkhas played as civilians can't be considered any lesser than their military cousins. They were the ones who cleared those inhospitable jungles, ravines, swamps, and hills to make it a liveable place for others; helped build roads and railways; worked in the mines; and helped establish new residences in remote locations of the northern, western, and eastern regions of India and stood firm as a security bulwark in the border areas.

Most importantly, the people of Darjeeling and Sikkim didn't appear anywhere as migrants; they have lived on the same lands from before the country was born. If they have remained there from the start, how can they be deemed as foreigners? They were (are) the sons of the soil, and sons of soil can't be called an outsider. This is the dilemma the people of Darjeeling are currently facing, and being named an outsider in your own home is undoubtedly one of the saddest situations.

The signing of the India-Nepal treaty in 1950 gave rights to the citizens of both countries to visit, work, and buy property in both countries enabling the citizens from both regions to enjoy the privilege for good since then. Over a million people from both sides are said to be working in opposite directions, although the official numbers reported by the Indian embassy in Kathmandu are much lesser. Over time, the open border policy has created an unprecedented problem of an identity crisis, especially for the Indian-domiciled Gorkhas. One is an Indian citizen, whereas the other is not. Still, there are no possibilities of differentiating the Indian and Nepali-domiciled Gorkhas, and people from the mainstream Indian communities often use it as a tool to bully the Indian-domiciled Gorkhas for their personal and political gains. Mixing them up and calling them names is cheap, petty, and wrong. Calling your fellow compatriots a foreigner is not acceptable, but they have been doing this to the Gorkhas for decades, hurting them in the process. The pain of living as an outsider in your own home is not something to joke about, and playing with people's feelings is like playing with fire. If not careful, it can burn the whole darn place down.

They are also tired of being a second-class citizen in their own country, and not having an Indian face forces them to prove themselves again and again and again. Why? *'For God's sake, we have been here for generations after generations.*

We have never left the place and know no home other than this one. Was that our mistake too?' They wanted to shout out but they have lost their voice as well, and may never make any noise again.

'We couldn't get Gorkhaland because of the 3Ts (Tea, Timber, and Tourist)', said one of our hosts in Darjeeling. He might have said it jokingly, 'after all, it's all about the economy, stupid!' but he didn't need to say anything else. Famous for its tea, the Darjeeling tea brand is one of the top varieties sold from India internationally. Darjeeling has an extensive timber industry, and its supplies of trees like oak, pine, teak, birch, chestnut and maple are standard here to meet the state's demands for wood and logging. Thanks to its beautiful green hills, serene tea gardens, cold and soothing weather, and the majestic Kanchenjunga Himal, Darjeeling has always been one of the top tourist destinations for both Indians and foreigners, attracting over a million visitors each year.

Additionally, the region is blessed with abundant herbal and medicinal plants and contributes significantly to India's pharmaceutical and Ayurvedic industry. 'The 3Ts alone are big time earners for the state, and without them, they would have abandoned us a long time ago. If this cash cow is gone tomorrow, they will serve Gorkhaland to us on a platter.' He summed it up succinctly, and we had no reason not to agree.

After the economy, experts have pointed out that security is another reason why the dream of the Gorkhaland has yet to be materialised. The region is strategically positioned and has common borders with neighbouring countries of Nepal, Bangladesh, Bhutan, and China, making it a zone of importance to national security. It also connects the Northeast region with the rest of India through a narrow corridor known as the 'Chicken's neck' that roughly stretches for 200 kilometres with a breadth ranging between 20-60 kilometres. Academics have highlighted that this corridor has been used by Pakistani ISI (Inter-Services Intelligence) as a supply route to provide arms and ammunition via Bangladesh to insurgents in the Northeast region. The Chinese could also drop Special Forces to choke the vulnerable corridor and cut off Northeast India from the rest of the country.

Furthermore, the corridor is the only route to transport foods and other supplies to the Northeast; a disruption in the passage could bring the entire region to the brink of a total disaster. The elites from New Delhi and Kolkata are also said to have an unfounded reservations about handing over such a strategically significant region to the Gorkhas, for they suspect the Gorkhas from both the area and Nepal could join and plot something sinister together against India.

However, the main shortcoming of the campaign is said to be coming from the Gorkhas themselves; many believe it has been the most damaging. The lack of an ideal, visionary, and charismatic leader from the Gorkha community; working on emotion and not on a campaign roadmap; and constantly fighting each other instead of the common enemy were some of the grievances heard at the meeting and experts had concluded the three main reasons why the campaign has failed so far. First, the lack of unity; second, they were too selfish by nature; and third, the leaders sold out cheaply.

The Gorkhas are renowned for their bravery around the world, but the leaders acted like a tiger in front of their people but turned into a mouse in front of national leaders in New Delhi. The sons of the brave Gorkhas have turned into a bunch of cowards. So-called intellectuals, journalists, influencers and community leaders are quickly sold out. They work on behalf of the state government, and help stop the community from uniting for a common cause. Whenever someone, whether a writer, politician, artist, businessman, or a person of influence, tries to come up with a good idea, these sell-outs come out in force and pounce all at once to pull them down. They never let the community integrate and become involved together as a whole. The selfish leaders of the Gorkhaland movement have ruined Gorkha's good reputation and made the community a laughingstock of the whole nation. In short, the Gorkha community is a victim of the crab-mentality experts pulling each other legs regardless of the benefits and motives.

The West Bengal government has applied the old divide-and-rule policy towards the Gorkhas just as the British had tested before in India. The initiation of the Development and Cultural Boards across the ethnic and community line, which further fragmented the community, is a typical example of the government's policy. Unfortunately, the people who run, promote, and execute those boards are the Gorkhas. People have accused the government of West Bengal of not doing anything to find a long-term political solution to the Gorkha aspirations besides selective, intermittent, and scattered development doses here and there, which neglected the

Gorkha people's feelings. The impositions of grievances of neglect, deprivation, injustice and exploitation in all socio-political and administrative arenas by the government have instead escalated among the Gorkha communities. The West Bengal government also used systematic discriminative measures in a number of policies such as those associated with school, language, and government jobs. Several Bengali schools outnumbered Gorkhali schools by manifolds, so much so that there were hardly any schools for the Gorkhali community in certain areas. Most government jobs also required spoken and written Bengali as a prerequisite skill that automatically ruled the Gorkhas out of the competition. Moving the governmental offices from the Darjeeling hills to Siliguri, where the Bengali has a majority due to the influx of Bangladeshi migrants, is another step of further alienating the Gorkhas from mainstream society in their place.

The rich and beautiful Darjeeling district has now turned into a moribund economy. The Bengalis own all the tea gardens, businesses, and vital institutions, and most of the tea gardens remain suspended in a skeletal state. Deforestation is severe, natural resources are almost used up, and developments have reached a standstill.

The situation in Darjeeling has deteriorated to such an extent that the people have started joking about it now. 'The British managed to bring a train up the hill, they couldn't even bring water now', they say, mocking their grim situation and joking here about the water scarcity.

The association between the movement's leaders and the BJP (Bharatiya Janata Party), the ruling party, has been going on for almost a decade. Not much happened during this period, and many said the Gorkha leaders were solely to blame for having nothing to show to their suffering people. 'Once the national leaders saw the movement's leaders from up close, the realised they were not up to the job and were doing just enough to get the necessary votes for the next election', one expert chided in. If the Gorkhaland demands are met, Gorkhas living in other parts of India, such as the Northwest and the Northeast, might raise similar requests sooner or later. The myth of 'Greater Nepal' is also used against the Gorkhas in all regions of India, alleging the ultimate goal of incorporating those areas into Nepal. Such a claim can be treated as a fantasy, but when tactically used by the media and political leadership, it can be a powerful weapon against the Gorkhas. As a result, the Gorkhas have become nothing more than a voting bank for the political parties, and they know how to use them.

I wasn't surprised when a rumour of the creation of a Union Territory comprising Araria and Kishanganj districts of Bihar, Darjeeling, Kalimpong, Jalpaiguri, Cooch Behar, and Alipurduar districts of West Bengal, and possibly parts of Kokrajhar district of Assam, tentatively named 'Simananchal' was reported in a local paper, and was said to have been discussed among the circle of stakeholders in the region. I heard a similar proposal from one of the respected persons who suggested the newly formed state will have a different name like 'North Bengal' or something else. What difference does it make as long as we get a new state? He explained. If such rumours are true, the aspiration of the Gorkhaland is over once and for all. Something good will come out of it for the Gorkhas from the region.

'Blaming others for everything is easy, but it won't get us, the Gorkhas, anywhere near our goal', another expert explained. 'The dream is not dead yet, though, it's flowing undercurrent now, but no political party can survive without the movement agenda in their policy', a third expert hypothesised, about the current situation on the hills. But they might have to wait longer than they had initially thought. Until there comes a leader (or a group of leaders) who is incorruptible and free of materials gains, loves Darjeeling and their people; has the experience, wisdom and courage to fight for the people; and has vision, charisma, and determination to lead the people out of this doldrums for good, things will remain unchanged. Until then, the people must endure and hope for the best, as put by one of my friends. I wish you all the best.

The Inevitable Impact on the Gorkha Community

As suggested before, the scope of this book is not to promote the past movements but to highlight the problems the Gorkhas have experienced because of incidents such as the Assam and Bodo Movements, also known as 'the Sons of The Soil Movement and the Anti-Foreigners Movement'. In the wake of identity assertions and growing ethnic conflicts in the Northeast region, unfortunately, the Gorkhas found themselves on the receiving end more often than not and suffered tremendously. The apathetic and indifferent policy applied by the state and the central authorities has been the cause of their suffering, and all sides have treated them unfairly despite living there for many generations. It also went against the India-Nepal 1950 treaty that guaranteed the protection of personal safety and property of people from both India and Nepal; thus, labelling the Gorkhas as foreigners and eventually evicting them from their homes was fundamentally wrong and unlawful.

The Assam Movement started during the 1979 election when the draft enrolments of the Mangaldoi constituency showed a high number of non-citizen voters, which had been a widely known fact since 1963 and the All Assam Students Union (AASU) and All Assam Gana Sangram Parishad (AAGSU) decided to start a campaign demanding India government to detect, disenfranchise, and deport illegal aliens from the state of Assam. After the government failed to heed their demands, the campaigners called for the closure of all educational institutes and picketing in state and central government buildings and polling offices, followed by a score of state-wide closures and rallies. The agitation continued for the next six years, costing hundreds of lives and causing the loss of properties and displacements for many people. The Gorkhas were one of the victims of this unfortunate event despite the Muslims of Bangladeshi origin being the protesters' primary target.

Although the Gorkhas have been living in Assam since 1826, the campaigners labelled the Gorkhali migrants as foreigners. Since India's independence, Bangladeshi migrants have been crossing the porous border and have resettled in various parts of the Northeast region, particularly after the Indo-Pak wars of 1965 and 1971. In 1971 alone, over ten million Bangladeshi refugees are said to have crossed to India, and Assam was one of the most affected states. Rattled by the influx of Bangladeshi migrants and fearing becoming a minority on their own home turf, the Assamese took the pressing matter into their own hands and started the agitation. The Bangladeshi were their first target and they committed the infamous Nellie and Khoirabari massacres, claiming 2191 (over 10,000 unofficially) and 100-500 lives, respectively.

The first time the Gorkhas faced a non-violence expulsion from their home was when the British evicted them from the Char (mid-stream sandbars) and Chapari (grazing reserves) areas. The other time was when the Kaziranga Reserve Forest was formed in 1920, when forest rangers and foresters burnt the grazer's households, causing harassment and considerable property loss. The British also removed the Gorkha settlers from the Naga Hills for demographic considerations during the colonial era.

During the Assam movement, it was here that anti-Gorkha feeling was first observed in Northeast India, and the Gorkhali communities were also labelled as foreigners alongside the Bangladeshis. Besides, the Gorkhas were not carpetbaggers; instead, they had massively contributed to the making of modern Assam through sweat, blood, and tears for centuries. The Assam movement saw unprecedented violence in various areas through demonstrations, collective threats, and sporadic attacks targeting mainly the Illegal Bangladeshi migrants that also forced the Gorkhas living in those areas to flee their homes. A substantial number of Gorkhas were also displaced from the regions of Choulkhow Chapori, Silapather, and Gohpur. Following the Nellie massacre, about 500 Gorkha families are said to have left for Nepal from Tezpur, Sonitpur, and various parts of Assam, and they then settled in the border areas of Kakkarvitta, Biratnagar, Dhulabari, and Dharan in Nepal. The rest resettled in Kathmandu, Pokhara and other cities in Nepal or returned to their original villages in other parts of Nepal.

During the Assam movement, Gorkhas from other states of the Northeast were also displaced from their home. Almost 60-100 families from Manipur, an unknown number of families from Nagaland, and a few thousand individuals from Meghalaya were displaced during the Anti-Foreigner Movement that spilt over to those states from Assam.

The Assam Movement that took 860 lives ended in 1985 after the Assam Accord was signed by leaders of AASU-AAGSP, the government of India, and the Assam state. Before peace could return to the region, another violent movement emerged in the name of the Bodo Movement in Assam and the surrounding states in the Northeast and found notoriety among its victims as the Anti-Foreigners Movement.

The Bodos are an ethnic and linguistic aboriginal tribe of Assam who inhabits the northern areas of Brahmaputra Valley in places like Kokrazhar, Udalguri, Chirang, Baska, Darrang, Sonitpur, Kamrup, Nalbari, Barpeta, and also found in various Northeast states like Nagaland, Manipur, Tripura,

Meghalaya, and Arunachal Pradesh. To protect their vested interests, the first political awakening appeared in 1933 when the Bodo community formed the All Assam Plains Tribal League (AAPTL) as a political party and demanded a linguistic identity. Two more political parties were formed in 1967, the Plain Tribal Council of Assam (PTCA) and the All Bodo Students Union (ABSU), demanding a Union Territory called 'Udayachal'. Being squeezed and outnumbered by the ever-increasing and overreaching influxes of Bangladeshi migrants, the Bodos felt their identity being threatened. They started fighting back to protect their way of life. With a new, young, dedicated Bodo leader, U.N. Brahma, the ABSU formed an umbrella organisation named the 'Bodo People Action Committee' (BPAC) and submitted a 92 points charter of demands to the state and central government of India in 1987. In its next annual conference, the request for a separate state for the Bodos and other tribals of Assam called 'Bodoland' was accepted by the ABSU and the entire Bodo community.

After a mass movement mobilised under the leadership of ABSU and BPAC for the next six years, the campaign finally ended with the signing of the Bodoland Accord in 1993. It formed the Bodoland Autonomous Council (BAC). The newly formed BAC failed due to its failure on border demarcation, and the frustration and anger forced them to come up with radical ideas and adopt violence. The Bodo Security Force (BSF), a militant force formed in 1986, was renamed the National Democratic Front of Bodoland (NDFB) in 1996 and had already resorted to violence and killings. At the same time, another militant outfit in the name of the Bodo Liberation Tigers (BLT) was formed and joined with ABSU, creating a two-outfit alliance with a clear ideological difference. If BLT wanted a separate state Bodoland within the country, NDFB asked to create a sovereign state out of Indian territories; thus, they fought each other. The fratricidal killing not only brought political setbacks but also threatened the peaceful existence of the Bodo people in the region. After the government's intervention, the two infighting sides agreed to sign for the Bodoland Territorial Council (BTC) to create a self-governing body for the Bodo areas in the state of Assam in 2003 to fulfil the aspirations of the Bodos relating to their cultural identity, language, education and economic developments. The extent of the BTC's jurisdiction is known as the Bodoland Territorial Areas District (BTAD), and the violent Bodo movement that killed thousands and displaced hundreds of thousands finally ended with the signing of the BTC.

Although the Santhals happened to be their primary target of the Bodo movement, the Gorkhas also suffered an unprecedented scale of harassment, extortions, mental tortures, evictions, displacements, and loss of lives and properties in Assam and other northeast states. Waged as the Anti-Foreigners Movement, the Gorkhas throughout the northeast region were unfairly targeted and brutally rooted out of their homes for almost two centuries. Outside factors such as the Gorkhaland movement in Darjeeling, the Bhutanese refugees' crisis, and the India-Nepal treaty of 1950 that had created an unwanted and false perception to all Indians that all the people with a Nepali/Gorkhali face were from Nepal, further impounded the matter and added more miseries to the already troubled Gorkha community. They have always been deemed an outsider despite their being in this land. The state government also had been playing a hide-and-seek game of inclusion and exclusion in its policies of protecting the rights of the Gorkhali communities. In 1947, they were given a 'protected class' status in the constitutions of tribal belts and blocks but were excluded in 1969. They were included again in 1984 with the RAP (Restricted Area Permits) issuing and again in 1996 as a vote-buying tactic. At other times, the exclusionary tactics continued with deportation and eviction of the Gorkhas from the region, marking it a serious issue during the agitation.

The other reason the campaigners targeted the Gorkha communities was its close connection with the security forces, especially to the Army. The rebels fighting the security forces suspected the civilian Gorkha communities of being informers. Since the Gorkhas occupied mainly those remote and scarcely populated tribal lands near the borders, they were severely affected by the ongoing fighting between the security forces and the rebels. They were accused of being a sympathiser by both parties. In the rage of revenge, the Gorkha communities were severely punished by both sides and had their villages burned down, causing unimaginable losses of lives, properties and domesticated animals. Families displaced by the fighting have been living in those makeshift shelters in inhumane conditions and still haven't been able to return to their homes for decades.

Many Gorkhas fled the region because of imminent harassment, threats of deportation, eviction and insecurity in their lives and properties. Houses and cowsheds belonging to the Gorkhas were burnt down; animals were looted, killed, and forcefully displaced from their livelihood. The Gorkhas population within the BAC wasn't significant, a mere 2.5 per cent, but their existence, along with the 63 per cent non-Bodos, constituted a considerable threat; thus, the Gorkhas were targeted and displaced along with the other non-Bodo communities. The hard-hit areas were Amteka, Patabari, Malivita, and Koila villages, where 20-25 Gorkhali households were displaced from each village. A similar number of families were evicted from Mangalchara and Khalasi forest villages.

The Anti-Foreigner sentiment also spilt over the nearby states, and the Gorkha communities suffered unprecedented injustice. In Manipur, the Gorkhas experienced direct attacks from the locals in 1980, forcing many to shift houses and flee to safer areas. Similar sectarian violence erupted in 1986-87 when the Gorkhas living in Shillong, Jowai and other parts of Meghalaya were directly attacked by the Khasi tribe by killing, burning Gorkhali villages and schools, and finally deporting the Gorkhas by the state government. Fearing for their lives, many of the Gorkhas fled, and the worst affected were the dairy farmers who had to give up their occupation when their cowsheds burned down and their cattle were looted. Gorkhali labourers working in the coalmines at Jowai were first targeted, and many children were said to have died of hunger because their parents didn't return home for weeks. The incident displaced over 150,000 Gorkhas as they fled their homes. Over 10,000 Gorkhas were living in seventeen resettlement camps in Shillong alone during the peak of the violence, while over 7,000 fled to Nepal. Most couldn't return to their homes as arsonists burned them down.

The Gorkha communities in Mizoram, Nagaland, and other states also faced the brunt of the agitation and suffered violence and eviction. Whenever there were border clashes between the security forces and the tribal forces in places like Nagaland and Arunachal Pradesh, it was always the Gorkhas who received the brunt of both sides in the end and suffered displacement and loss of livelihood in many incidents.

In the aftermath of the Assam and Bodo movements, there is a deep feeling of insecurity, frustration, and helplessness about the situation among the Gorkhas in the Northeast. The situation also helped re-examine their position and a need for an assertion of the Gorkhali identity, resulting in the formation of various Gorkhali organisations. Currently, they have the Gorkha Development Council (GDC), the Gorkha Autonomous Council (GAC), the All Assam Gorkha Students Union (AAGSU), and many more that help protects, promote, and advocate for various issues related to the Gorkha communities in the region.

When we visited the Raid Marwat village at the Assam/ Meghalaya border, I figured out why the Gorkhas became an easy target whenever conflict broke out. The Gorkhas were the first to settle in cities like Shillong and Guwahati before they sold the places cheaply and moved further to the outskirts of the cities. They preferred living nearby the jungle with their animals. They were also disorganised, always acted individually, and needed more unity and cohesiveness. They also hadn't learned the importance of keeping proper documentation in their possession and failed to provide those necessary documents when required. The rapid urbanisation of the land forced them further deep into the jungle of the tribal lands, creating friction between the tribal people and the Gorkhas as one got accused of encroaching while the others felt threatened. It's also quite surprising and disheartening to see villagers like Gopal Bhujel at the Raid Marwat village, whose forefathers had migrated here as a cow-herder, and not much has changed in the last two hundred years. Suppose 200 years are not enough for you to change. In that case, Gorkha villagers like Gopal Bhujel will always end up as the whipping boy of the community, and the bad days for the Gorkhas in the region are, unfortunately, not going to be over anytime soon.

The Bhutanese Refugee Crisis

After the signing of the Sinchula Treaty on 11 November 1865, the Anglo-Bhutan war 1864-65, also known as the Duars War, ended. With it, the lower plains of Bhutan, known as Assam's Duars and Bengal's Duars, were ceded to the British, and the British started bringing many Gorkhali people to work there. The southern parts of Bhutan were scarcely populated by then, mostly with thick jungles, ravines and hills, and needed a sturdy hand like the Gorkhas one to clear them and pave the way for cultivation. They were mainly farmers and cow herders. As they had already been doing to other parts of Northeast India, the Gorkhas came in big numbers with their animals, grazed the land, cleared the jungles and slopes, and created new terraces where they grew crops. The British encouraged the Gorkhas for security, demographic and economic reasons and found them a readymade and willing solution to all of their pressing problems. Just like the ones at nearby Sikkim, Darjeeling, and Assam, the Gorkhas community flourished here in Bhutan, and they had been living there for generations as the locals since then.

Bhutan is a kingdom ruled by the Wangchuk dynasty since 1907 and had signed a treaty with the British in 1910, granting them control over Bhutan's foreign relations. After signing a similar pact with independent India in 1949, Bhutan has come under India's security umbrella, and India, as Bhutan's primary donor, has been guiding its foreign matters since then. Bhutan implemented its first citizen act in 1958, granting full citizenship to people in southern Bhutan, including the Gorkhali community.

Bhutan embarked on its first modern 5-year plan in the 1960s, attracting many Gorkhas from Nepal to work in construction and other fields. By the 1980s, the Gorkha community made the majority in southern Bhutan and spread over different parts of the country. The Gorkhas, also known as 'Lhotshampas' (the southerners), had their school, practised religious and traditional rites, and lived a separate way of life that differed from the majority Buddhist Bhutanese.

When a new citizenship act was passed in 1985, and a new census carried out in 1988, it clearly showed the swelling number of the Gorkhas, making up one-fourth of the entire population of Bhutan. Although officially put at twenty-eight per cent, the unofficial estimated as high as 30-40 per cent of the total population and triggered an alarm of urgency within the ruling elites. Like a multi-fanged cobra, the most significant threats came from politics, religion, and culture. Barring the Gurungs, Tamangs and Kiratis, the Gorkhas practised Hinduism in a Buddhist Bhutan. The Gorkhas also tried to import political awareness into the country. Feared being outnumbered in their own country, the King initiated a cultural identity policy called 'One Nation, One People', requiring people to practice Buddhism, wear a traditional northern dress in public and adopt their customs, teach the Bhutanese language in school, and promote and preserve folklores used in the new year and marriage celebrations, house blessings, and archery contests. As a result, western clothes were banned, the teaching of the Gorkhali language in school stopped, discouraged Bhutanese from marrying non-Bhutanese, and those found breaching the royal decrees were subjected to heavy fines and jailed.

The final crackdown came in 1989 when the Bhutanese

government implemented the Citizenship Act of 1985, which explicitly required the Lhotshampas to produce a land tax receipt specifically from 1958 as proof of their status. Many failed simply because of the carelessness in Gorkha's nature. They couldn't provide one as required, rendering themselves reclassified as illegal immigrants by the government, facing uncertain futures and eventually deportation. Facing the sudden rise of discrimination and the government's unfair crackdown, the Gorkhas united and made their voice heard through protests, rallies, and demonstrations. The ongoing liberation movements in Darjeeling and other parts of the northeast region also affected them. The anti-government protest marches rocked the nation; calling the Bhutanese government a 'cultural suppressor', the leaders charged the government with human rights violations, including torturing prisoners, arbitrary arrest and detention, restriction on freedom of speech and press, and worker's rights.

As the clashes between the security forces and the anti-government protestors intensified, houses and shops were burned, and bridges and vehicles were blown away by remote-control bombs. The Bhutan People's Party, reportedly established by antimonarchists and backed by the Nepali Congress and the Marxist-Leninist faction of the Communist Party of Nepal, was branded by the Bhutanese government as a terrorist organisation and accused of being armed with rifles, guns, knives, and homemade grenades. They were also allegedly involved in activities such as disrobing people wearing Bhutanese national dress, extorting money, robbing, kidnapping, and killing people in southern Bhutan. The clashes between them and the security forces are said to have killed more than 300 people, wounded 500, and resulted in more than 2000 arrests.

Tek Nath Rizal, a former member of Bhutan's National Assembly who established the Bhutan People's Forum for Human Rights in Nepal, was said to have been abducted in eastern Nepal by the Bhutanese police and taken to Thimpu, the Capital, where he was imprisoned on charges of conspiracy and treason. The other organisations involved in the movement were the Bhutan Students Union and the Bhutan Aid Group-Nepal.

But the terrors it had brought to the Gorkhas community were unimaginable as schools were closed and post offices, police, health, forest, customs, and agriculture posts and buildings were destroyed, bringing people's livelihood virtually to a halt that forced many of them to flee their home. Tens of thousands of Gorkhas were expelled or fled from Bhutan, and most ended up in eastern Nepal refugee camps. In 1990-1992 alone, over 80,000 Gorkhas arrived in Nepal and recorded more than 108,000 refugees by the end of 2000. Nepal had seven refugee camps during the peak of this unfortunate crisis under UNHCR's supervision and up to 600 people a day arrived in the camps in Nepal. The departure was almost one-sixth of Bhutan's total population, making it one of the world's largest migrations by population.

The government of Nepal and Bhutan established the Joint Ministerial Committee (JMC) in 1993 to verify the status of the people in the refugee camps and to work out toward a resolution of the refugee crisis. After conducting seventeen meetings over the next ten years, nothing changed

for good. Although Nepal had sought India's participation in the talk, India ruled itself out, stating that the refugee crisis is a bilateral issue between Nepal and Bhutan. Despite international pressure, Bhutan ignored the international calls and continued its suppressive policies against the Gorkha communities. Lands owned by displaced refugees were distributed to landless people from northern Bhutan, and those who remained in southern Bhutan continued to face severe and sustained discrimination and persecution. Since 1991, the Gorkhas have been required to get 'No Objection Certificates' to declare that neither they nor their relatives were involved in any anti-government movements. The certificate is needed to access schools and other government services, work in government offices or gain a business license, and sell other cash crops.

Amid the pressure from the international communities, Nepal and Bhutan formed a Joint-Verification Team (JVT) consisting of Nepali and Bhutanese representatives and started screening the status of 12,173 inhabitants of Khudunabari camp in 2001, of which 75 per cent of those screened were found eligible for return to Bhutan. Repatriation was expected to start with the completion of the verification, but the Bhutanese halted the process after a physical attack against the JVT members in 2003. After the incident, the Bhutanese team returned to Bhutan, and no formal talks between the two countries were ever held again. The negotiation failed after the Bhutanese King declared in 2005 that those in the refugee camps were not Bhutanese citizens and could have been living in Nepal or India previously, closing all the possibilities of the refugees returning to Bhutan once for all.

On the contrary, a quick survey conducted by the camp organisers in 2010 found a completely different status in the camps. Out of the total registered refugees, 84.65 per cent had Bhutanese citizenship certificates, 10 per cent had land ownership certificates, 2.95 per cent held school, marriage, court and services certificates issued by the Bhutanese government, and only 2.35 per cent didn't hold any identification papers which they alleged that Bhutanese government officials have forcefully seized from them.

That Nepal was also going through a difficult time didn't help the refugee's case. The Maoist insurgency was at the pinnacle of its fight against the ruling party in Nepal and infiltrated and formed several Maoist groups inside the refugee camps. With the growing Maoist ideology among the refugees, the U.S. and the international community expressed concerns about such a trend and started resettling them outside countries by 2006. Under the management of the International Organization of Migrations (IOM), a U.N. agency, the first batch of refugees totalling about 5,300 individuals, settled in the U.S., Australia, Canada, Denmark, the Netherlands, New Zealand, and Norway by September 2008. The resettlement process of the refugees to overseas countries continued in the coming years, and by 2016, 104,010 of them had already resettled in eight countries overseas.

According to a spokesman from UNHCR, as of September 2022, 113,500 individuals have resettled worldwide, and only 6365 individuals have remained in the remaining two camps (Beldangi, Damak - Jhapa and Pathai-Sanischare, Morang) in eastern Nepal. In Mid-July 2022, we passed by the Beldangi camp on our way to Kathmandu from Northeast India and found the centre quiet and relaxed. With no security checking at the gate, it was an open camp allowing everyone to come in and go out freely and found a small group of people (all Bhutanese refugees) gathered in front of the main office. The person in charge of the camp had yet to arrive, and the people waited there chitchatting. Barring some grocery stores and convenient shops alongside the road, the base mainly seemed empty and rarely managed. Despite not being monitored or supervised by any officials, I could quickly notice their wary faces tinged with signs of suspicion, distrust and discomfort, and we didn't attempt to talk with them. I also learned from the locals that they had been allowed to take some jobs in the neighbouring town, and it didn't look like a refugee camp at all as far as I was concerned. After a while, it started raining, so we left the camp hastily. As I prayed for a way out to the remaining ones in the centre, I wondered what would happen to those who had settled alongside the road leading to the camp when the camp finally closed.

Before the refugee crisis, the Gorkhas comprised about 35 per cent of Bhutan's total population. After displacing more than 135,000 Gorkhas, the number has gone down drastically in recent years, and they make up only about 20 per cent of Bhutan's today's population. The Gorkhas still live under systematic and sustained discrimination from the Bhutanese government today. One could hardly believe that the Bhutanese government could have perpetrated such cruel and inhumane treatment to the Gorkhas without its protector's blessing—the big and powerful India. The role India played during the crisis's height further proved its position. When the eviction started, and the Gorkhas fled their homes in masses, India was the first safe place they landed on. But instead of dealing with the crisis and taking care of the refugees, the Indian military loaded them into the truck, drove them to Nepal's border, and dumped them there, leaving no chance of having a single refugee inside its border. India's action breached not only the international refugee protocol and human rights but also the principle of ethics in our society as humans. By loading those helpless refugees in trucks and dumping them in front of its tiny neighbour's door, India tried to wash its hand, tarnishing its position as the big brother of south Asia.

Under the veil of its Sangrila, as a peace-loving nation image and a so-called Gross National Happiness policy, Bhutan has been able to conceal its atrocities against the Gorkhas so far. But history cannot be hidden for too long. Those Gorkhas displaced by the cruel Bhutanese government have resettled in various parts of the globe, especially in the USA. Over 20,000 Bhutanese currently live in Ohio State alone, creating a substantial number of united communities and organisations that have already started raising their issues through leading international media and powerful institutions. The remittance money those people send back to their relatives in Bhutan is also increasing over the years. They also hope for the Bhutanese government to recognise their contributions to the country and accept them as Non-Resident Bhutanese (NRB), so they can return home freely someday soon, and the entire nation can reconcile for good and live together happily after. And I, for one, would like to wish them all the best.

In 2023, a group of high-profile Nepali politicians, including a Bhutanese leader, were embroiled in a court case and taken into police custody. They were accused of registering several fake refugees in return for a large sum of money. At the time of writing, the accused were still fighting the court case against them while remaining in police custody, and the case has undoubtedly harmed the Bhutanese refugee's reputation in the international community.

The Implications of the Indo-Nepal Treaty 1950

The Indo-Nepal Treaty of Peace and Friendship, signed on 31 July 1950, has become a subject of debate and resentment both in Nepal and India from the beginning. The autocratic Rana oligarchy that ruled Nepal from 1846 to 1951 ended after the signing of the Tripartite Delhi Agreement in 1951 between the Nepali King, the Ranas, and the Nepali Congress in Delhi. The Indo-Nepal Agreement was further revised in 1956, and despite many calls for a review, over the years, it has still been in effect as of today. In recognition of the historical values and connection of the two countries and safeguarding peace in the region, the signing of the treaty established a framework for the unique ties between the two countries. The treaty has ten articles, and a separate letter of exchange kept secret from the public by the Ranas until 1959. All those treaties previously signed between the British and Nepal were cancelled through article 8, for they had no place in a post-British India.

Critics from both sides of the border have their motives, and the answer varies on which side you have been talking to. 'Nepal has benefited more from the treaty' if you ask the Indians, they won't miss a chance to remind you. A Nepali would mostly say, 'it's an unfair treaty, and we should ask for a review'. But Nepali people primarily expressed dissatisfaction with article numbers 2, 6, and 7, widely discussed among intellectuals, scholars and ordinary people. Nepali politicians have also raised the issue from time to time without any results simply because they had been nothing more than political gimmicks used spuriously only during elections.

After the British were gone, the Rana regime, which survived only because of the British's help and backing for the last 105 years, suddenly found itself alone and vulnerable and urgently needed to have the newly formed India on its side if they were to continue ruling Nepal. The Ranas were desperate and ready to sign their acceptance to any terms to hang on to power. The exchange of a separate letter with the treaty that they didn't make public until 1959 was the first reason why people suspected them. That Mohan Shumsher JB Rana, the then Prime Minister of Nepal, signed the treaty as the head of state. In contrast, Chandreshwar Prasad Narain Singh, his opposite side who signed on behalf of India, happened to be just an ambassador, also gave critics another dose of suspicion, for they were not of an equal footing which showed a clear sign of India's affront towards its smaller neighbour. Furthermore, the Ranas, for not being democratically elected by the people, couldn't have represented the people of Nepal—they argued.

The international community then was dominated mainly by the capitalist, communist, and non-aligned nations. India needed Nepal under its security umbrella as a buffer zone between itself and communist China. India was disturbed by China's adventurism in Tibet and worried about its possible influence in Nepal, Bhutan, Sikkim, Ladakh and NEFA. India also needed Nepal to be under its confidence to secure its northern frontier. In other words, both countries signed the treaty for their own needs and got the best out of the deal, at least at the time of signing.

The secret letter between the two governments was about Nepal's agreement to give first preference to the Indian government or Indian nationals in development projects related to national resources and setting up security posts on the northern border. Nepal also agreed to buy arms for the Nepal army use through India. India had seventeen military posts alongside the Chinese frontiers in the Himalayas exclusively operated by the Indian Army until they were removed by the then King Mahendra in 1959. All of the public roads, bridges and other infrastructures built before the 1960s were constructed by Indian contractors. The letter also made it possible for Indian companies to hold the rights of all the projects involving Nepali rivers, making it another reason why the Nepali public resent the Indians.

Nepali people feel short-changed with this treaty because the Ranas, who fully accommodated India's security and commercial interests, had long lost their power. Still, the treaty they had signed survived till today, to the chagrin of the whole of Nepal.

The first issue raised regarding the treaty was in 1969 when India failed to inform Nepal before the war with China in 1962 and Pakistan in 1965, a clear breach of article 2, which required India to consult with Nepal and adopt the best solution in case of any serious friction or misunderstanding with any neighbouring countries. In a clear display of its attitude towards Nepal, India didn't consult with Nepal again in the Indo-Pakistan War of 1971 involving the making of Bangladesh as a new country, which showed India's hubris and total disregard towards Nepal. With it, India's promise of fair treatment as equals to Nepal was consigned to words only but has never transpired in action since then.

People also believed that article 6 favoured the Indians more than the Nepali businesses, giving unfair advantages to Indians. Indian business people have a monopoly in all forms of business in Nepal. They also captured all the rights over Nepal's rivers, giving another reason for growing mistrust and discontent among the general public in Nepal.

King Mahendra tried to balance out India's influence in Nepal by extending Nepal's co-operations with China and other western nations. He also invited experts from the US and other western countries to work in various fields such as education, agriculture, infrastructure, and other areas of development within Nepal.

After his death, his heir King Birendra adopted a non-align policy in Nepal and gave continuation to his father's policies. India didn't like it, for they had/have an allergy to the word 'China' and hated everything about it. The first friction between Nepal and India came in 1989 when India ordered an economic blockade on Nepal that lasted for almost 13 months. Disagreeing on a trade deal was the reason for the embargo, immediately closing 19 out of 21 border entry points between the two countries that crippled the landlocked country like Nepal with no viable economy of its own and three out of its four sides bordering India. The real reason behind India's action was Nepal's growing involvement with China and its recent buying of Chinese military arms and equipment without consulting India. King Birendra also dared to dissociate the Nepali rupee from the Indian rupee, which freely circulated in Nepal before. In return, India stopped processing the importation of goods in Kolkata for Nepal, thereby holding goods coming to Nepal from other nations than India.

The Maoist insurgency started in 1996 also demanded a revision of the treaty in its 40-points demand. The Communist Party of Nepal (UML) also promised to review all the treaties in its manifesto in the 2008 election. All the left and communist parties of Nepal called India's treatment of Nepal a borrowed British legacy from its colonial era, thus, hegemonic and imperialistic. In 2008, then-Prime Minister Pushpa Kamal Dahal called for scrapping the treaty and reviewing several other treaties regarding the principal rivers of Nepal. But most of such calls demanded by the Nepali leaders have mainly been limited to only talks but no actions, for they were mainly aimed for political gains and quickly forgotten once the razzmatazz of the election fever was over.

Still, article 7 of the treaty (exact words: that grants, on a reciprocal basis, to the nationals of one country in the territories of the other the same privileges in the matter of residence, ownership of property, participation in trade and commerce, movement and the additional benefit of a similar nature) that heralded an open border policy between the two countries had/has become the most controversial one. If Nepal has a million people working in India at a time, over 600,000 (official figure, the actual figures are in manifolds) live and work in Nepal. Mostly migrated from the nearby Bihar and Uttar Pradesh (UP) states, over six million Nepali of Indian origins live in the southern plains of Nepal, also known as the Terai, making up about 20-25 per cent of Nepal's total population. Known as the 'Madhesi community' in Nepal, whereas men from the hills are called the 'Pahadis', the Madhesi makes up almost 96 per cent of the total population in Terai, and the two communities hardly mix. The Pahadis are suspicious of the Madhesis and see them as a proxy for India's hegemonic and expansionist ambition to control Nepal. Madhesi political leaders didn't even pretend to be otherwise and ostensibly carried on hobnobbing between New Delhi and the state capital in Bihar and UP for power and support.

The skeleton came out of the closet in 2015 when the Madhesis started a protest movement against the authority for not being fairly represented in Nepal's newly promulgated Constitution. The agitators blamed the Nepali government for socio-cultural and administrative discrimination, economic exploitation, and political exclusion, and the struggle had already been going on for almost a decade. When the government failed to appease the Madhesi's demands and openly sided with the Madhesi demonstrators, India started an economic blockade on 23 September 2015 that lasted six months.

When the Indian-domiciled Gorkhas faced a similar fate in both the Assam movement in the 1980s and the Bodo movement 1990s and suffered ethnic persecution, burned their houses down, looted their animals, and unfair eviction, India did nothing to protect them and left to die. India's indifference, apathy and ambivalent policy towards the persecuted Gorkhas gave away their double standard in handling the situation involving the people of Indian and Nepali origins - passive for the Gorkhas and active for the Madeshis cause. India's failure to protect those displaced Gorkhas also violated article 7 and further fueled the irrelevance of its provision within the Nepali people. Making Sikkim the 2Second state of the Indian Union in 1975 further fuelled Nepali people's suspicion towards India and gave birth to conspiracy theory like this one—a small country like Nepal can be overrun by demographic means alone, for Indians breed very fast. The influx of Indians to Nepal could squeeze us out of here in no time.

Another pricking issue between the two countries is the recent border dispute at Lipulek, Kalapani, and Limpiadhara of west Nepal, a strategically important tri-junction between India, China and Nepal and an ancient trade route India closed after the Sino-India war 1962. India reopened it in 2015 after constructing a 22km road for Kailash Mansarovar. Indian side claimed Nepal has a problem with the village called Gunji from which the road has started. But the Nepali side claimed the whole areas of Lipulek, Kalapani and Limpiadhara to be its territories and issued a new map showing the disputed territories. This flared up the old dispute between the two countries, and the nationalists went for each other's throat, at least verbally. The situation calmed down after the then Nepali Prime Minister KP Oli had a secret meeting with the head of RAW (Research and Analysis Wing of India's Foreign Intelligence Agency), Samant Goel, in Kathmandu, and nobody talked about the new map again.

Article 7 of the treaty created an unprecedented identity crisis in Nepal and India. After Pushpa Kamal Dahal, the leader of the Communist Party Nepal (Maoist), visited New Delhi in 2022; his coalition party initiated and passed a controversial new citizenship law from the parliament, which the country's president refused to sign and was eventually shelved after it did a few more rounds between the parliament and the president's office. Had it been passed as a new law, many new Madhesi brides would have obtained Nepali citizenship within a week or month of their marriage. The fiasco was shelved after a massive public outcry, and the leader's credibility took a beating as a sell-out. But such displays of utter disgrace or charade by political leaders in Nepal are nothing new, for Nepali leaders are notoriously famous for such lowly and shameless behaviours. The country is the last thing they have in mind.

Similarly, the Indian-domiciled Gorkhas are also suffering from the same acute identity crisis for generations on the other side of the border. Unlike the Madhesi community in Nepal, they never had powerful politicians on their side, thus having to deal with the problem on their own. Despite living in India for generations, the Indian-domiciled Gorkhas have to prove themselves again and again, for the mainstream Indians put them all in the same basket by calling them Nepalis. They are Indians of Nepali origins, have been living here in India for generations, and didn't come here by choice but have been living here in their land. There is a big difference between Nepali migrant workers of Nepali origin and the Indian-domiciled Gorkhas of Nepali origin, and calling them all with the same name is wrong and unfair to them. This misunderstanding (knowingly or unknowingly) has created an enormous problem, unnecessary stress and harassment, and unprecedented discrimination against the Indian-domiciled Gorkhas, and the sufferings are devastating.

And every time the dispute between the two countries escalates, it is the Indian-domiciled Gorkhas on the other side of the border who always face most of the brunt of this unfortunate issue and faced tremendous pressure, harassment and abuse regularly. We will discuss this particular issue in detail in the next chapter.

The idea has been floated since 2014. Nepal and India finally agreed to review the Indo-Nepal treaty of 1950 and formed a team of four experts on each side in 2016. The Nepali review team, called the Eminent Persons Group (EPG), was led by Dr Bhekh Bahadur Thapa, whereas Bhagat Singh Koshiyari led the Indian team. Although the EPG concluded the report in 2018, only a little has happened since then. Indian Foreign Ministry has acknowledged the report has not yet been submitted to the Prime Minister after four years. The Nepali EPG team also talked about making the report public but still needs to do so. Experts believed India's dissatisfaction with the report was why they were not proceeding. Others suggested India never wanted the treaty review in the first place. They agreed only because India needed Nepal's support to become a permanent member of the UN Security Council. Once that time of need has passed, they no longer have to adhere to that term. It clearly shows the reality of the India-Nepal lopsided relationship where nothing ever happens without India wanting it, and the fate of the review of the India-Nepal Treaty 1950 is as good as it's been shelved for the time being. The Nepali side could do nothing about it, which gives another reason for the Nepali general public to resent India's big brother policy towards weaker Nepal.

The Gorkha's Loss of Identity

The British did a good job making the Gorkhas world-famous. But that was only one side of the story, for they had ulterior motives. The over 200-year-old Grokha institution made Nepal poor, dependent, and hollow, as nothing has changed since then. Gorkhas are scattered worldwide, mostly in countries like Singapore, Hong Kong, and the UK, and are having an identity crisis today. New generations living in those foreign countries need to learn more about Gorkha's history and have no sense of connection with the Gorkha institution. They feel uncomfortable calling themselves Nepali, too, for they haven't lived enough in Nepal to understand and value the culture, tradition and way of life there. Most of them cannot even talk a proper Nepali, let alone read and write, and the only thread that keeps them hanging there is that they originated from a place called—Nepal—that's all.

The situation of the Gorkha communities in both Hong Kong and the UK might be mild as of now, for they started migrating there between the late nineties (Hong Kong) and late 2000s (The UK). They may still have some more years before it gets worse. The identity crisis the Gorkhas are facing in India is much more serious. Gorkha communities living in other parts of the world can learn crucial lessons from them. Humans have followed certain traits for centuries, which are relatively easy to find if we carefully study them. We always found safety and strength in the majority, and the locals are always the mainstream community that always takes the significant share of the cake when society prospered. As a result, the new migrants always start as a minority, making them the whipping boy of the community and forcing them to live on leftovers. The only way to survive and thrive in such a situation is unity, but this is what the Gorkhas have always found lacking.

The loss of identity crisis the Gorkhas are currently facing in India is severe, unfair, and unfortunate. The stereotyping, biased, disgraceful, and discriminatory treatments the community experiences daily are not only undeserved and unwarranted but also wrong, and the mainstream community, as well as relevant authorities, are to blame for the continuation of such unaccepted treatment of its people for so long. Despite having innumerable problems of their own, outside factors played a significant role in the making/breaking of the Gorkha's fate in India, and the India-Nepal Friendship Treaty of 1950 that propagates an open border policy between the two countries is considered to be one of the leading causes of their ongoing problem. As described in the previous chapter, article 7 of the treaty allows citizens from India and Nepal reciprocally visit, work, buy property, and run a business in both countries, respectively. As a result, over a million people from both countries live and work over the opposite border, creating an unprecedented identity crisis for the people of both Nepali and Indian origins who have been living there for generations in their respective countries.

Over ten million Indian-domiciled Gorkhas of Nepali origin face the identity crisis daily, and they blame the open border policy as the leading cause of their ongoing trouble. It has become so toxic that people want to tear it off by their hand if possible, and cancellation of the open border policy has become one of the main demands of Gorkha movements since then. It all started with a mere name, name-calling that is, forcing people to wonder what's in a name anyway. But the consequence can be fatal when the nation starts calling you a specific group or race of people by a name, especially a derogatory one used to put you down. This is precisely what the Indian Gorkha communities of Nepali origin face daily in today's India, struggling to find a way out of this unfortunate and unnecessary dilemma.

Besides Nepal, a considerable number of Nepalis live in Bhutan, Sikkim, West Bengal, Assam, Meghalaya, and Manipur in the Northeast region. Similarly, a substantial group of Nepali communities also live in Jammu and Kashmir, Himachal Pradesh, Uttarkhand, Uttar Pradesh, Bihar, and other parts of India. They are Indian citizens of Nepali-speaking people called the Indian Gorkhas and have lived in India for over two centuries. Indian Gorkhas is the term used to differentiate between Gorkhas, who are Indian citizens and Nepalis citizens, who are allowed to stay and work in India as per the open border policy of the Indo-Nepal treaty 1950. This fact got mixed up as the mainstream community started calling them all Nepali, adding an identity crisis to one of their fellow countrymen - the Indian Gorkhas.

By calling them (both Nepalis from Nepal and Indian-domiciled Gorkhas of Nepali origin) all Nepali, unknowingly or unknowingly, the Indian mainstream communities have inflicted unnecessary pain, indignity, and humiliation on the Indian Gorkha communities. The Indian Gorkhas have been subjected to various discriminatory remarks and name-calling and have been unfairly treated since then. Even politicians of the very high office have spoken out against the Indian Gorkhas with contempt, calling Nepali a foreign language that added fuel to the already worsening situation. The whole country still thinks the Indian Gorkhas of Nepali origin, whose mother tongue is Nepali, fall into the servant class and Bollywood, the tinsel town of the filmy world, contributed a great deal to cement that image by portraying all the Gorkhas in stereotyping roles such as a Chaukidar, a driver, or a servant - calling the Gorkhas 'Bahadur' had become disrespectful now which used to be respectful before and made the mockery of the word itself that the Gorkhas had earned with a display of unparalleled bravery in both WW1 and WW2. Nepali migrant workers working in those lowly paid jobs such as street cleaners, porters, house servants, delivery boys, road and construction workers, toilet cleaners, and security guards with inhumane conditions didn't help improve the general perception the mainstream communities have about the Gorkhas. The continuous trafficking of Gorkhali women to the brothel of India's sin cities further tarnished their image.

"Not having an Indian face is not a crime, and being born with a Mongoloid face, slanted eyes, and fair complexion won't make you a foreigner. Despite living here legally for generations, why do we have to prove that we are Indian citizens repeatedly? Why do people tell us to go back to Nepal? We didn't cross the border; borders crossed us instead. We didn't come here alone; we came with the land. This is our home; we are the sons of the soil here, and yet, why do we have to prove our identity again? We never moved; we have been here on our land since we knew about it. Why don't you get it? How can a man become a foreigner in his own home? Why should we go to Nepal? For we have nothing there, know nobody there. And we will be called a foreigner there in Nepal, but not here, at least that I have known for life". Those are not the words I have made up to fill up the pages here, but a list of genuine comments I heard from real people during our research trip to India. I didn't know ABCD has a different meaning here, which means Ardali (servant), Bawarchi (barber), Chowkidar (security guard), and Driver, and the real intention behind using those words. The crisis has become so severe in some states in the Northeast region that some Gorkhas have to hide their identity by naming their children after their mother's surnames and stop speaking the

Gorkhali language at home and outside. They are adopting drastic measures to survive, and one must do what's needed in such a desperate situation.

They were genuinely concerned, utterly frustrated, and determined to make their voice heard. Out of this frustration, helplessness, and being unfairly treated, they started speaking out, giving way to popular movements such as the Gorkhaland and Lhotshampa movements in Darjeeling and Bhutan, respectively. To crawl out of this mess of identity crisis, having a separate state of their own like the Gorkhaland became a life-or-death matter for the community; many were ready to sacrifice their lives for the cause. The Gorkhas had the suspicion of their state and central governments for not being fair to their communities. The relevant authorities had always taken the communities for granted and ignored their plights. The government's unsupportive policy of indifference, apathy and ambivalence was fully displayed during the Assam and Bodo movements. The campaigners openly singled out the Gorkhas as foreigners, killed their animals, burned down their houses, and displaced them from their homes in many states from the Northeast region. Instead of protecting the victims, the state government stood alongside the campaigners, and the state police shamelessly helped evict the Gorkhas from their villages. And this has been the main policy that the authority has applied towards the Gorkha communities since then; unfortunately, thus expecting otherwise from the relevant authorities is pretty useless. A good lesson for all, but as for as the Gorkhas are concerned, the penny hasn't dropped yet for good.

The anguish of being called a foreigner in your homeland is not funny at all. One couldn't comprehend it until they have experienced it alone, and one shouldn't wish for this to happen to anyone, including the Gorkhas in India. The identity crisis the Indian Gorkhas are currently facing is their own making as much as caused by outside factors. If the communities were united, leaders were not selfish and cheaply sold out, and had nurtured a leader of impeccable charisma, vision, and selflessness, their suffering would have already stopped long ago. They hadn't had to beg for rights that were rightfully already theirs. Until that happens and Indian national leaders start taking the community seriously, nothing much will change, and the identity crisis facing the community will continue for some more time. On a consolation note, this can be a case study for other Gorkha communities around the globe, especially in Hong Kong and the UK, and help avoid repeating this unfortunate situation for good.

The Gorkhas started migrating to Hong Kong in the 1990s when the British left Hong Kong before 1 July 1997.

The British retained only 2,500 out of 10,000 Gorkhas, and the rest were dispatched home. Instead of returning to their villages and becoming village chiefs in Nepal, as put by the British, the discarded Gorkhas came to Hong Kong. They started working in security, bodyguards, transportation, construction, and many others. By the 2000s, Hong Kong had a sizeable Gorkha community consisting of veterans and their families. Thanks to their excellent reputation, getting a job in Hong Kong was easy for the Gorkhas. Gorkha children also got residency rights through birth, making Hong Kong Gorkha's favourite destination after Nepal.

After the groundbreaking announcement of 2009, when the British Gorkhas and their families won the right to abode in the UK, the Gorkhas living in Hong Kong started migrating to the UK. By 2020, most British Gorkhas had shifted to the UK, primarily leaving the Second and Third generations of Gorkhas in Hong Kong. Currently, around 29,000 Nepalis are still living in Hong Kong and are known as one of the ethnic minorities in the city.

As of the 2018 census, about 110,000 people of Nepali origin were living in the UK, of which 78 per cent were of the Gorkhas and their descendants. The Gorkhas mostly live in Aldershot (the UK's army town) and nearby areas such as Reading, Swindon, Maidstone, London, and other parts of the UK. Within a decade of settling in a new country, they have improved a great deal and are involved in various fields of society. If the old generations work on security, transportation and labour, the new generations work in medical, education, service, and IT (information technology) industries. A small number of the community have also tried and flourished in business, and the Second and Third generations are scaling up the education ladder. In a nutshell, the Gorkha communities in Hong Kong and the UK are doing great, at least on a personal level, and that's okay for the descendants of the Gorkhas who knew nothing other than soldiering.

But when the question comes on a collective basis as a community, the situation could be better than it is individually, and maybe it's time they do something about it. The identity crisis that the Indian Gorkhas are facing today will sooner or later catch up with them and decide their fate based on the decision they have taken today. The identity of a person or a community is much bigger than people's achievements, and failure to heed and work on such a significant matter is like an inviting disaster. Unity among the community, understanding the big picture and working cohesively and persistently towards realising that goal of identity are keys to avoiding that situation. The Gorkha communities in the UK and Hong Kong have less than 30 years to save themselves.

The Gorkha communities will have three names to choose from—The British (Or Hongkongers in Hong Kong), Nepali, and the Gorkha). It won't matter much whichever term you select, for each will have pros and cons. You can become a hardcore British, but the shell will come cracking when an adolescent punk full of acmes in his face shouts at you something like this—go back to your fucking home in Asia, wherever it is. Calling yourself a Nepali won't make you comfortable as you don't even speak the language, let alone read, writing and understand its history. And using Gorkha won't cut it, too, as it's not related to any caste, tribe, or creed of people but just a term created by the cunning British for their convenience.

Moreover, Gorkha is somewhat related to military personnel, and one cannot stick to it forever. But in the end, it doesn't matter what name you choose to call yourself as long as you are comfortable with your identity. A British of Nepali origin or a British Gorkha of Nepali origin—what difference does it make? What matters the most is that you know who you are as a community, and other people and the communities around you recognise and respect you. Still, if you need some inspiration, look at our big neighbours—China and India. They have 'China Town' and 'Little India' in many parts of the world. Please help establish something like they did in both Hong Kong and the UK and call them "Gorkha Village' or 'Little Nepal'. If the community can do that, that will be more than enough.

'Muglan Pasnu', or going abroad, is not a new word in Nepal, for Gorkhas have been going abroad for over two hundred years. Yet, they still failed to learn one vital lesson and faced the consequences more often than they should have. Whenever you migrate to a new country, you automatically become a minority, meaning you will have to survive doing all the odd jobs, be discriminated against in every aspect of life, and work double harder than the locals to get a real chance in life. In other words, you are the whipping boy of the mainstream community, and unity is the only way to get out of that position. You unite and work as a team, make your own identity, and have your representative from the ground level. It doesn't matter how low it is, neighbourhood committee, village committee, district committee and so on. You start from the very bottom and climb until it reaches a certain point from which your voices will be heard by the entire community and, eventually, the country. Only then will your

future in the new country be secured, which should at least be the minimum target of all the newly migrated communities, including the Gorkhas.

But as far as the Gorkhas are concerned, they always seemed to have a different idea of what this lesson was all about and failed to heed them. The first thing they always do in a new country is to open a new organisation and add more. It started with a family-related one, followed by caste, village, hometown, hobby, school, political party, work, the old Gorkha regiment they served, and so on. Before long, there will be hundreds of organisations in a small community. For instance, there are almost 400 organisations within the 29,000 Gorkha community in Hong Kong. They are also mired in internal bickering and infighting for limited resources and personal rivalry. Some of the so-called community leaders don't even see each other eye to eye, let alone unite and work together for the sake of the community. Most are selfish, disorganised, and narrow-minded and have no intention other than serving their ego and lack.

Whether they live in India, the UK, Hong Kong, or other parts of the world, it doesn't matter as they all work the same way. Lack of unity, being too selfish and selling out for cheap are the main reasons the Gorkhas have consistently failed as a community. Foreigners like the British, Indian, American, European, and Asian, and Rulers from the Gulf nations have already learned about the Gorkha's weaknesses and know how to treat them. And this is the main reason why the Gorkhas have been used, mistreated and exploited by so many countries and still haven't found a voice to speak up against it, let alone set themselves free of this modern era of slavery. For God's sake, it has been over two centuries; maybe it's about time you guys wake up!

★ ★ ★

The Stigmatisation of the Gorkha

Being a citizen of one country and serving in the army of a different country is not an ideal position that one could ever feel proud of, and finding oneself in such an unenviable situation is not only anarchical but also unfortunate. The Gorkhas are one of those communities around the globe who falls into that undignified category and still carry on the legacy without a whiff of grievances for a little over two centuries. Renowned as the best and bravest soldier in the world, if you believe in the British uppity of nonsense, the Gorkhas have been serving in the British army since 1815 to the present day. The other institutions where the Gorkhas still render their services today are the Indian army, Singapore Police, and Security in Brunei as the remnants of the British colonial era and inherited from their past colonial master.

No matter how superficial it was, the British propagated flattery that worked as magic for the thick, simple and illiterate Gorkhas and enslaved for over two centuries. The Gorkhas community was so grateful to the British that they treated the British as their saviour and willingly sacrificed their sweat, tears, and blood. The association of the British and the Gorkhas have been so successful that it has become legendary within the British army's history. The legacy continues today as it was 207 years before. Yet, the Gorkha's history, loyalty, bravery and dedication couldn't avoid the stigma that came with the name and failed to shake off the mercenary tag that had ruined its good standing for years. The word mercenary becomes a synonym for Gorkha, which is very unfortunate.

Calling the Gorkhas mercenaries is premature, for the topic is much more complicated than you might think. One must always remember that unlike the actual mercenaries, who are usually hired for a particular and short-term job, the Gorkhas are enlisted in the regular national army for the long term with a pension. Furthermore, they also got hired through the provision of an international treaty signed by the involved countries that have been ongoing for the last 207 years, making the practice of becoming a Gorkha a tradition and a way of life. An institution that lasted for over 207 years cannot be called mercenary, thus comparing the Gorkhas to a mercenary or labelling them as one of such is not only unfair and wrong but also an insult, and one should try to understand their history first before jumping to a conclusion. It also shows how ignorant people are. Despite legally serving in a national army, why did the Gorkhas have to go through the stigmatisation of this mercenary tag then? If they had done nothing wrong, why do they have to experience such indignation and humiliation? The answer lies in people's ignorance, pettiness and bitterness. I, for one, as a community member and a product of the Gorkha institution, who has experienced it firsthand, I am proof of such bias and injustices. I am here to tell you of its ugliness as it is.

The Gorkhas might be excellent soldiers, but they are not a learned or educated bunch. They would have never become good soldiers if they had been in an academic community. Lacking awareness in this department is the main reason the Gorkha communities suffer such insult, indignity and unfair treatment. Even worse, those who were supposed to protect the Gorkhas are the ones who are responsible for all those abuses and gave a bad name to the excellent and innocent Gorkha people. It's the British, the Indians, the Nepali elites, and the ignorant bunches who played significant roles in harming the Gorkha's reputation by calling them mercenaries and causing irreversible damage to the Gorkha's otherwise good name. Betrayed by their people, the Gorkhas have no choice but to blame their destiny and toil. When you have friends like this, who need an enemy? It feels like sayings like this were made only for people like the Gorkhas, and trust me, I wasn't complimenting them.

It won't be an exaggeration if I say this—the British never get tired of reminding the Nepali people how good friends they have been. But trust me, they are anything but your friend, for they are Nepal's friend only because of the Gorkhas. The Gorkhas were extremely useful to the British and came cheap. And that's the only reason they are nice to Nepal—take the Gorkhas out of the equation, and everything changes overnight. As the saying goes—action speaks louder than words, and let me explain how the British's actions didn't match their words.

As the British extended their rule over India, they needed a strong army to protect their newly acquired territories, and the Gorkhas fitted the role. The Gorkhas were brave, loyal and obedient. Most importantly, they were cheap, costing only one-tenth of the Europeans, and there wasn't a single war in which the Gorkhas didn't shed blood for the British. When the British left India in 1947, they shared the Gorkhas between the British and India as one of their most precious bounties and reaped the benefits as of today at the expense of a poor country like Nepal. They even conducted the signing of the tripartite treaty in 1947 between the British, India, and Nepal in a dubious way. To avoid the mercenary tag in the future, Nepali Rana Prime Minister requested a guarantee from the British, asking for an equal term on ranking, promotion, salary, and other welfare of the Gorkha soldiers compared to their peers in the British Army. After leading him to a separate room for a private talk, the trios eventually signed the treaty. But the

Nepali Prime Minister's demands later appeared among the footnotes of the signed treaty, giving room for allegations that the British and India had already agreed on the final terms leaving no room for Nepal's unexpected terms to be added to the treaty. Thus, the British had to offer something privately to appease the Nepali Rana Prime Minister.

There was a massive discrepancy in how they treated the Gorkhas compared to their British army counterparts. Despite being served under the same British crown, we had two separate systems—one for the Gorkhas and the other for the rest of the British army. Pays, allowances, medical and other welfare, training system and facilities, rules and regulations, and everything you name it. I, for one, had served in the British army for 13 years and witnessed firsthand experience. Compared to other British soldiers, our training was more demanding, rules and regulations were stricter, and even our holidays and weekends were strictly regulated. In our battalion in Hong Kong, we had a couple of British other ranks (Bors) who were never subjected to any rules and regulations of our regiment. As a result, the British officers and Bors would never be seen after office hours.

In contrast, we, the Gorkhas, had to abide by many other rules, such as playing sports, evening lectures, extra classes, drinking sessions, light-out practices, and many more. And when it came to paying and other allowances, the Gorkhas had almost nothing except the basic pay, which was just a little over one-tenth of the British soldiers. There was also a discrepancy in promotion, a Gorkha could only promote to a Gorkha major, no commissioned officer, and every Gorkha had to build up his army career from a very low position as a Rifleman.

Among all the discriminations, the most derogatory and disgraceful one was the policy where a Gorkha major, the most senior Gorkha in a battalion with no less than twenty-eight years of service, had to salute a twenty-year-old British Second lieutenant, who had just joined the regiment after finishing his officer's training course at Sandhurst, UK, and was with the same age as the Gorkha Major's son. One could only imagine the senior officer's indignation, but the British never gave a damn about it. In a Gorkha battalion, the British officers were and acted like a King and treated us, the Gorkhas, as their private servants. It was more or less a master-servant relationship, and their sense of superiority over the Gorkhas made them rude and arrogant.

Despite being used, mistreated, and exploited by the British for the last 207 years, Nepal's respect and trust for them never diminished. Instead of asking for explanation and reparation, Nepali elites put them on a pedestal, making them even cockier. The British knew the power and influence they had over Nepal. They can virtually get away with almost anything. They are aware of Nepali people's mercenary nature and have no hesitation in treating them like one. The British were the first to learn about that weakness and have exploited it fully since then. First, it was in the British Indian army, then to Northeast and Northwest India, followed by Malaysia, Singapore, and Hong Kong. As of that, it was the British who first made us, the Gorkhas, a mercenary and calling us by that name was no coincidental. Therefore, we shouldn't be surprised at all by their actions. After all, it was what they were; failing to recognize them in their natural face was our mistake, and we are just paying for our own mistakes.

The British officers started trading off the Ex-Gorkhas as mercenaries in Brunei, Hong Kong, Iraq, Afghanistan, and other war-torn countries through employment agencies. They hired tens of thousands of them for a particular time. After retirement, those cunning British officers opened several employment agencies and hired ex-Gorkhas from their old regiments. They benefited greatly by sending those poor Gorkhas to dangerous places around the globe. This clearly showed the British played a massive role in making the Gorkhas mercenaries and Nepal a poor country.

After the British were gone, the Indians inherited the readymade country, a readymade army, including the Gorkhas, and all the power, position and problems that came with the government. Learning the old tricks from their past colonial master was nothing of a problem for the Indians, including the British colonial mentality and the tried and tested methods of using, misusing and exploiting the Gorkhas was one of them. Over time, the Indians, the new master as far as the Gorkhas were concerned, turned out to be cleverer, cunning, and sharper than the old master, and the stigmatisation of the Gorkhas as mercenaries further continued. Even worse, the Indian politicians have found the Gorkhas as a new tool to gain their political mileage and never hesitated to exploit this newfound tool. Instead of being grateful for their loyal service and fighting their wars at the border, Indian politicians and their cronies have insulted the Gorkhas with derogatory names such as mercenaries, foreigners, and parasites and openly called for them to be sent back to Nepal. Indian diplomats openly boast about the generous pensions, medicals and welfare facilities India has provided for the Gorkha pensioners in Nepal and make it sounds like they have done a favour to the poor Gorkhas. Instead of respect and appreciation, India patronises the Gorkhas, making them feel unwanted and unvalued. And by doing so, the Indians are proving to the Gorkhas that they are no better than their old master, the British and helping continue the same old policy that would never help liberate the Gorkhas from the stigmatisation of the mercenary tag.

Nepali elites' roles in stigmatising the Gorkhas as mercenaries were the opposite of what the British and the Indians had played. If the British and the Indians were active, the role Nepali elites played could be described as passive, for the British and the Indians did all the work for the Nepali elites that they had nothing else to do at the end. Nepali elites' inaction, indifference, ignorance, and negligence made the job easier for the other two sides. The British and the Indians did virtually nothing regarding the Gorkhas, yet the Nepali elites would not have said a word against it. You must be one of us, the Nepali, to understand why they would display such a mentality of utter indifference, apathy, and even cruelty. It's a type of mentality that can carve out only after living in a society where everything, such as religion, caste, tradition, backwardness, superstitions, neighbour activities, animals, gods, goddesses, and much more, matters to them except yourself. Not to mention the little jealousy, selfishness, greed, power, and position that come with being a human being, and we Nepalis are no different. We also enjoy pulling the legs of our people, for we need to be better at competing with other people anyway.

Most importantly, we don't care what happened to the other guy as long as we are fine here; we love power without responsibility, and the welfare of the country and the well-being of its people are the last things we have in our minds. And by the way, what's wrong with being called a mercenary anyway? You have food and clothes and get paid for doing your job. If you don't like it, move away, there are so many others to take your place, anyway.

Becoming a Gorkha is still considered one of the best jobs in Nepal, and the mercenary tag that comes with it won't deter any. Over 20,000 young men compete for 200-250 positions offered by the British army yearly, exposing a grim unemployment situation in Nepal. As this shows, becoming a Gorkha is still the best choice for youths in Nepal, and that's the reality. For them, becoming a Gorkha and being called a mercenary is better than it sounds. Instead, not having a choice to that choice is the worst and an unfortunate one. Until the situation in Nepal improves for good, we Nepalis will have no choice but to live on with the mercenary tag for now and hope for the best in the coming future.

On the bright side, living with a mercenary tag is better nowadays than before. After all, there is a price for everyone and everything in this world of globalisation, and everybody flaunts their speciality for a fee. If the rich and famous and most prominent names in sports, academia, celebrities, and many from other fields could be sold out for money, why can't the Gorkhas? They are simply doing it for a better life for their family. Besides, they were supposed not to be in that position anyway. Had they not been betrayed by their leaders and their so-called friends (British and Indian), they wouldn't have been in this situation in the first place. The British, the Indians and the ignorants are the ones who are to blame for this entire despicable act and should be condemned by all. If you have friends like them, who need an enemy, anyway?

The Gorkha Justice Campaign

Despite not being its colony, the British come to Nepal every year, take its best youths they need, and make them fight their dirty wars. Nepal is like a private water station for the British. They open the water tap, take whatever amount of water they want, and close it until they need more water again. And they have been doing it for the last 207 years, and nobody has ever asked a question about it. Isn't that great?

Two hundred seven years are not a short time by any means, for not less than ten generations would have gone in that period, and its implications on Nepal as a country were colossal. Yet, the British were not alone in this two-century-old crime; Nepali Rulers were mainly to blame for this disaster. Because they had weak knees for the British, they could give anything to the British in return for a photo opportunity with their British friends and sold the whole Gorkha community out for a pittance. In other words, Nepali Rulers were complicit with the British and must bear half of the responsibility for the Gorkha's miseries. The Ranas treated the Gorkhas as their personal property and used it to the fullest to stay in power. The rest of Nepal's Rulers valued the donation money more than the Gorkha's well-being. In a nutshell, the British committed discrimination of a historical proportion against the Gorkhas during the last 207 years, and yet, nobody uttered a single word against them.

The period I am covering here was between the aftermath of the Second World War and right before 1 July 1997, when Hong Kong, the last British colony in Asia, was eventually returned to China. With the return of Hong Kong to China, the need for the Gorkhas in big numbers also came to an end. Only a small number of the Gorkhas went to the UK as a part of the British Army for the first time. It was also the same period when the British treated the Gorkhas more cruelly, and the Gorkhas still suffer from the repercussions even today. It started right after the end of the Second World War when over 60 per cent of the Gorkha's total forces were sent home empty-handed. The subsequent culling came in 1969 when the British left Singapore and Malaysia for Hong Kong, and over 7,000 men (almost 50 per cent of the total force) were dismissed. The last mass dismissal came in 1994 when Hong Kong returned to China, and only 2,500 out of 10,000 Gorkhas were retained, sending the rest packing home back to Nepal. For being unfairly dismissed and not adequately compensated, the Gorkhas' main grievances against the British had been those dismissals, and they have been fighting against inequality, unfair treatment and discrimination the Gorkhas had suffered in the last seven decades.

The first Gorkha voice of discontent, distrust, and disparity against the British came in the early 1990s when Gorkha Army Ex-Servicemen Organization (GAESO) started a campaign asking for equal pay, pension and fair compensation. The campaign didn't do well initially, as sceptics and doubters stayed away and watched from the sideline. Only after the campaign had gone international it picked up momentum, and so were the numbers of its supporters. Meantime, other similar Gorkha organisations sprouted out within the community and joined the campaign. The first break of the campaign came in 2004 when the Gorkhas won a case initiated by the British Gorkha Welfare Society (BGWS), another active member of the movement in the UK, that gave the Gorkha the first-ever right of settlement in the UK, opening up more possibilities for the suffering Gorkha communities in the coming future.

Things started brightening for the Gorkhas once Joanna Lumley, the famous British actress, joined the campaigners. The actress's father, Major James Lumley, was a British officer who served with the Sixth Gorkha Rifles and was saved by Tul Bahadur Pun VC during a battle in Burma during the Second World War. Her admiration, connection and respect towards the Gorkhas didn't allow her to watch helplessly from the side, prompting her involvement in the campaign. The actress's involvement attracted media attention, and other dignitaries and famous individuals joined the movement. After collecting more than 250,000 public signatures, she handed it over to the government and applied more pressure on the UK government through various platforms. After a long and successful Campaigning, the UK government finally relented and made a historical announcement on 21 May 2009 that allowed all the Gorkhas and their children the right to abode in the UK. The Gorkha Justice Campaign started in the early 1990s and finally ended, and ten of thousands of Gorkhas and their families have settled in the UK since then.

Unfortunately, the historic settlement didn't solve all the Gorkha's grievances as they had hoped. Some organisations from the Gorkha communities have also accused GAESO of compromising Gorkha's demands by accepting lesser than they had asked. Instead of settling the pay and pension discrepancy between the Gorkhas and their peers in the British army, the UK government went for a less expensive solution and opted for giving out the right of abode. As a result, the historical grievances of discrimination and inequality persisted. Even worse, new problems emerged for Gorkha pensioners living in the UK. Their meagre Gorkha pension, which was only one-tenth of their British counterparts, was not enough to live a dignified life in the UK. The Gorkha communities genuinely felt cheated, for they seemed to have wasted the last 20 years of hard campaigning for nothing.

After the announcement, the Gorkha Justice Campaign almost halted, and everything seemed to swipe under the celebration carpet. The decision also divided the Gorkha organisations, giving birth to splintering groups in the community. Due to internal fighting, mismanagement and corruption, GAESO exists only as a skeleton. In contrast, BGWS has become a viable business entity serving the Gorkha community in the UK. Many other pretenders have come and gone, but the Gorkha veteran's core issue of pension inequality and other allowances remains unsolved today as it was 32 years ago. But the fighting is not all lost and gone yet and continues today. Thanks to a diehard Gorkha campaigner, Gyanraj Rai and his organisation British Gorkha Satyagraha United Struggle Committee (BGSUSC) and their supporters, the fight is still not over yet, and they are all here to keep on fighting for another day.

As I have already indicated earlier, the fight they had continued was for equality in pension, severance pay, and other allowances to those Gorkha veterans who had served under the British after WW2 and before 1997. Gyanraj Rai became a prominent Gorkha activist after he staged a solitary hunger strike at Whitehall, near Downing Street, in 2013 that lasted for 15 days. He stopped the hunger strike only after he received an official assurance from the government that his plights of the Gorkha veterans would solve once and for all. A technical team that would look after all the Gorkhas' grievances was duly formed and conducted a series of talks between the Gorkhas and the British government since then. Thanks to MoD's (Ministry of Defence) delaying and divide-and-rule tactics, they have been simply talking (on and off) since then without any result.

BGSUSC demanded more talks, but nothing substantial came out of it before the pandemic struck hard, bringing everything to a screeching halt. BGSUSC submitted a 12-point demand to MoD in early 2021. My book AYO GORKHALI has just been published almost a year, and people credited the book for saving the Gorkha Justice Campaign, for the book has all the materials they needed to resurrect the Gorkha campaign. The campaigners also repeated their demands and increased their voices against the MoD but were flagrantly ignored, forcing the organisers to go ahead with their next plan. BGSUSC started a relay-hunger strike in front of 10 Downing Street (The British Prime Minister's office) in July 2021. When they received no response from the MoD, the campaigners opted for an extreme measure—two Gorkha veterans and a Gorkha widow (Gyanraj Rai, Dhan B. Gurung, and Pushpa Rana Ghale)—and started a fasting-unto-death strike on 7 August 2021. The event attracted national and international media and garnered support from local and global communities. The London Metro Police used all the dirty tricks to harass and deter the Gorkhas and allegedly physically abused the three hunger strikers. The Metro police even took away their chairs and umbrellas and made them sit on the ground. Yet, undeterred and unruffled, the trio persisted, forcing the MoD eventually to agree to a talk and stop the hunger strike on its 13th day for good.

The joy and jubilation of the Gorkha community didn't last for that long. After the first meeting, the meeting reached a standstill for various reasons. Unprecedented problems started piling up one after another—for there were regime changes and political upheavals in both UK and Nepal, ambassadorial changeover, a pandemic, and the Ukraine war. As if the historical delays over seven decades (counting only after WW2) were not enough, the Gorkhas had to wait for more. When the pending talk finally resumed almost a year later, on 3 November 2022, a nasty surprise awaited the Gorkhas. To the utter dismay and disbelief of the Gorkhas, the MoD insisted on talking only about the Gorkha welfare back in Nepal. Instead of starting a serious discussion, they spent precious time on why the MoD won't speak on pension as the Gorkhas demanded from the beginning. After they fixed the next meeting on 21 November 2022, it was postponed to 30 November, and the dates kept changing.

The MoD was on its old game of delays, excuses, and divide-and-rule tactics again and had many tricks in its sleeves, which have been its main tactic of avoiding the talk and eventually shirking away from its responsibility. The Gorkhas have a timetable of ending the dispute by the end of March 2023 and pressing for an urgent discussion. But the MoD, as usual, however on its dirty old tricks again. They have taken the Gorkhas for granted for two centuries. They have no respect or regard for the Gorkhas and do everything possible to escape it. The MoD, thus the British, want to have all the cake for them and eat it, too. The delaying tactics also have another sinister side. The Gorkhas veterans involved in this case are already getting older, and the British don't want to settle the Gorkha issues before they are all gone. And the British are using another Gorkha entity, Regimental Associations, to help achieve their ulterior goal.

Regimental Associations are groups mostly made up of members from the old regiment, and they usually gather once/twice yearly. It's run mainly by the old guards of the unit, such as the Commanding Officer, Company Commanders, and the Gorkha Majors. They formed primarily for the sake of the old days and kept the same form and hierarchy as when they were in active service. As they used to do in their old regiment, those high-ranking officers keep bossing around the junior-ranking soldiers and NCOs (non-commissioned officers). Those Gorkha officers never went against the wishes and commands of the British officers, as they owed their promotion much to those very officers. The British officers came to Nepal yearly as most of such events were held in Nepal and got treated like Kings by the Gorkhas even after they had retired for years. For the sake of old days and memories, having a yearly reunion or get-together is common and more than acceptable. But as far as the British are concerned, that's always not the case. The only reason for the continuation of Regimental Associations is to have a tap on the Gorkha community on behalf of the MoD so that they could use it in negotiation with the Gorkha justice campaigners and the adaptation of their future policies. In other words, they were doing the bidding for the MoD and used to undermine the very interests of the Gorkha community.

A team of high-ranking British officers visited Nepal just a week before the talk between the MoD, and the Gorkha's representative was to resume. The trip was on for a fact-finding mission, and the MoD needed a briefing from the team to act as they had. It showed how the cunning British were using the Gorkhas against each other and trying to undo all the good works some community members had done so far. How ironic and pathetic. Until the community understands this issue and rises above it, Gorkha's problems will remain unsolved.

As I write this page, a third meeting between the MoD and the Gorkha representative took place on 15 December 2022, and the dates for future talks still need to be fixed. In short, the talk is still going on, and Gorkha's issue still needs to be solved. The discussion will continue and will be solved once and for all as they have expected by coming March 2023. And everyone can forget about the historical discrimination the Gorkhas have suffered so far and move on for good.

By December 2023, despite conducting a few more meetings between the two sides, they were still far apart, and the aim of solving Gorkha's grievances once and for all still remained a far-fetched dream.

The Nepal Situation

With almost 30 million populations, Nepal is considered one of the poorest nations in the world and 25 per cent of its people still live under the poverty line. Nepal's primary economies are agriculture, tourism, workforce, and other small industries such as carpet, textile, cigarette, cement, and brick. Nepal imports almost everything it needs from outside, especially from India. Without a reliable and stable industry of its own, jobs are scarce, and unemployment is its biggest problem. Nepal has around 16 million workforce, one of the highest globally, and youths with new aspirations and dreams of a better life flock to the cities in significant numbers. Heading to a foreign land for a better opportunity has been a century-long tradition for Nepali youths. The Gorkhas today serve in the national armies like the British, India, Singapore, and Brunei. Soldiering apart, Nepali children have worked as labourers in various Gulf nations, Malaysia, Japan, S. Korea, and many more. Over 6 million Nepali youths currently work in foreign countries, including over a million Nepali workers in India alone, sending money back home and making Nepal one of the big receivers of remittance money worldwide.

Nepal received almost US$10 billion, over 26 per cent of its GDP (Gross Domestic Product), in remittance money from its youths working overseas in 2021 alone. That's the official version. Experts estimated it to be around 36 per cent of the GDP as Nepalis mostly use an illegal way (known as *Hundi*) of sending money home. I have spent most of my adult life overseas and can say from experience that that number should be much higher than the official figure. I have hardly seen anyone send money through Nepali banks for one reason. They didn't have that service, and everyone had to send money through *Hundiwalas* or bring it along in person, either gold or cash, when they returned home. Therefore, that number has to be over 40 per cent.

Nepal was virtually a military state until 1951. While the people were in the dark for over 105 years without education, the Rana oligarchy and its followers indulged in very high life and plundered the nation's assets. To finance their expensive lifestyle, the Rana oligarchy levied high taxes on the people, primarily poor and needy farmers with prominent families. They struggled to feed their families and pay the tax simultaneously. To avoid prosecution and in search of better land, they started moving eastward and migrated to as far as Sikkim, Darjeeling, Bhutan, Assam, and the Northeast region of today's India. It was not by choice but desperation that forced people to migrate, and Nepali people have been doing so for the last two hundred years. To understand this phenomenon better, one only has to look at the long queues of Nepali youths in front of the Tribhuwan International Airport in Kathmandu heading to foreign countries.

Nepal is known by the outside world for three things— the Himalayas, Lord Buddha, and the Gorkhas. When Nepal started opening in the early 1950s, it was a mysterious country with only a 2 per cent of literacy rate. People just wanted to be here and experience this new Sangrila nation with high mountains, making tourism its primary industry for apparent reason. Nepal has eight out of ten top mountains worldwide that are over eight thousand metres high. The first ever tourist visa was issued in 1955 by King Mahendra. They started with hippy tourism, adventure tourism, and spiritual tourism. Tourists poured in without having to do much from the authority, adding the Himalayas are here, so here they come. Buddhism is big in Asia, especially in Japan, Korea, China, Vietnam, Thailand, and Cambodia. Lumbini, Buddha's birthplace, can be a huge tourist attraction with proper facilities, management, and promotion. But Nepali nationalism only goes as far as shouting a slogan such as 'Buddha was born in Nepal', and that's all. And as far as the Gorkhas are concerned, the Gorkha community should be lucky if they are not looked upon with contempt by the country's elites, and that's all there to be said about them.

Of the significance of its geographically strategic position, Nepal had the attention of the world's powers from the very beginning. India and the west needed a buffer zone between them and the expanding communist China. They found a new Nepal more than willing and showered it with money. Nepal had to ask, and the men delivered the money. Once upon a time, Nepal received so much money from donors that they didn't know where to spend it. They invested in all sectors, such as education, politics, roads, hospitals, bridges, factories, and many more. But not much improved in people's livelihood, nor did Nepal's overall situation as a country. The donors might have come with good intentions. Still, they failed miserably for a reason, for the westerners had no regard whatsoever for the needs, understanding, and requirements of the Nepali people. All they did was impose their own social, political, religious, and educational ideologies that were too foreign to the Nepalis and thus wholly useless. They were like paper houses built on the air—all glitters but no substance. Even worse, the damages it had done to the process of nation-making were colossal, and Nepal didn't recover from it again. What happened was that the donor's policy did spoil the Nepali elites to the core; they failed to establish a strong foundation for institutions that helped develop a nation and ruined its future. Nepal has become too dependent on foreign donors, and its new generations are paying the price daily for the old generation's mistakes.

Nepal, as a country, has gone through many ups and downs since then. But only the country's elites have tasted the fruits of the country's labour and benefited greatly. The Maoists' ten years of insurgency (1996-2006) killed, maimed, and displaced tens of thousands of innocents from their villages. Inundated by the fleeing villagers with harrowing stories and nightmares, cities like Kathmandu valleys, Pokhara, Dharan, and all the regional centres of Nepal became overcrowded, overpriced and unsafe. With virtually no industries of its own, an unstable economy, and unreliable governance, unemployment became rife; thus, seeking a job in a foreign country became the only option the country's youths had, making human resources Nepal's only export so far.

The brutal killing of the then King Birendra and his entire family (Queen Aishwarya, Crown Prince Dipendra, Prince Niranjan, Princess Shruti, and other members of the royal family - altogether ten people) on 1 June 2001 was one of the darkest days in Nepal. The massacre not only devasted the whole country but also signalled the ending of the Shah dynasty that had ruled Nepal since 1767. Moreover, King Birendra was one of the most beloved kings of Nepal, and people had genuine admiration and affection for him. The official version made the Crown Prince Dipendra culprit, for he got so upset and angry at his parent's refusal for him to marry an Indian Princess that he got drunk and killed them all off in a moment of madness. But of course, people didn't buy it as the case seemed much more complicated than the officials wanted people to believe. Conspiracy theories started making rounds among the general public. Rumours had it that the King's brother, Gyanendra, who became the King later on but abdicated as the last Shah King of Nepal in 2006, was to blame, while others say foreign powers such as India's intelligence agency and CIA were involved as they were not happy with the late King's non-alignment policy and needed to get rid of him. Perhaps people might never know the truth, but one thing was clear—the monarchy in Nepal had gone once and for all.

As if that was not bad enough, Nepal is crippled with corruption, unruly and bureaucratic civil servants; selfish and narrow-minded leaders; unreliable and rapacious government officials; useless and outdated educational system; and careless, naïve, and ignorant citizens who sell their precious votes in exchange for a cup of tea or a meal. The country has become so reliant on outside donors that nothing ever happens without outside help. Unlike other countries, members from foreign embassies, INGOs, and other institutions openly get involved in Nepal's internal affairs, and one can hardly meet a person in Kathmandu valley who has no connection with these foreign institutions. Advertisements offering services and contacts of the agencies who deal with employment in foreign countries like the US, Canada, Australia, Japan, Europe and so on are displayed almost everywhere. Youths in Kathmandu study just enough to qualify for a foreign student visa, whereas the parents eagerly wait for their children's eighteenth birthday so that they can send them outside to a foreign country. Worse, while in Kathmandu, one couldn't miss the sense that everybody is on the move with one foot already up and over the door and ready to get out of the country on the first chance they could get. It makes one wonder how we have come to this point.

Nepal has always been a client (vassal) nation for the world's superpowers. Before, it was to stop communist China, now, it was to contain powerful China, and that's the only difference. One can blame the world, but Nepal's people are responsible for all their woes today. But nobody would have ever pointed a loaded gun at them if they were not so willing, and one has to look no further than the traffic mess in Kathmandu. You have buses, trucks, cars, tricycles, motorbikes, cycles, and pedestrians all go simultaneously, they come and go from all directions, and nobody follows the traffic rules. One word to describe this mess in Nepali is *'Bhadragol'*, chaos in English. Kathmandu's unruly, dangerous and reckless traffic mess represents not only its traffic situation but also the country's overall situation and how you wantonly disregard rules and regulations as a citizen. It's not about how you drive a car or behave on the road, it's all about you, and it tells everything about Nepal.

Furthermore, every road, bridge, or public infrastructure is made with a proper plan in Kathmandu valley. Unlike many other countries, where they carry out a feasibility study, field report, and final approval before proceeding with the plan, they do things here differently. For instance, to have a new residence, they find land first, divide it into small plots, sell it to potential buyers, build houses, and move in. They will only start looking for roads and bridges to connect with the city centre and find schools, hospitals, grocery and hardware shops, post offices, police stations, fire stations, and so on. Critical structures such as drainage and sewage system are the last thing they think about, and by the time they realise it, it has already been too late. Everything is for a quick profit. If you don't believe this, I suggest you go to the Kopan monastery hill, look back at the valley, and see how near the city centres like Dharahara and Tundikhel are to your position. You ponder that it could have taken less than fifteen minutes in a taxi. Yet, the actual ride takes almost an hour; why? Because there is no direct route as expected, and it has to take a long detour via Chabahil, and the traffic is horrible.

The infiltration of party politics in every society, institution, and government department is another disease that's eating the country from the inside out. The politicisation of the governmental institutions is rotting the whole system and making ordinary people's life horrible. One has to be a member of this or that party to get a job, promotion, or anything done. Life has already become harder for those without a party affiliation, and it has further polarised the society that has already been affected by caste, religion, race, superstition, and communal beliefs. Its long tentacles have reached even outside the country and affected Nepali Diasporas around the globe, creating unnecessary division with undesirable consequences.

The Maoist insurgency that started on 13 February 1996 and ended on 21 November 2006 was undoubtedly one of the most painful times in Nepal. Although the armed movement might have been created with good intentions, it gave people nothing but pain, misery and suffering, and history shouldn't be kind to those who have mishandled the movement. By bringing class wars between the rich and poor, they struck the cord of Nepal's core social problem and won big, at least personally. The ten years of conflict killed over 17,000 people, wounded another ten thousand more, and displaced hundreds of thousands of innocent villagers. Despite all those sacrifices, unfortunately, the Maoists have nothing much to show in the end. The only achievement the movement has gained was a golden entry for its leaders to the mainstream political party that guaranteed unimaginable power, money and position for them and seven generations after them. By destroying poor men's sons and daughters, they have secured their life for ages and never uttered a word of remorse or regret about those who sacrificed for them. What made it even more painful was that those Maoist leaders hailed from the ruling castes, whereas those killed and displaced were primarily the children of the Janjaatis. The Maoist movement was supposed to help the poor and underprivileged; instead, it piled more suffering into their already miserable lives. People considered the Maoist insurgency one of Nepal's mistakes and wished it could be forgotten as a long and undesirable nightmare.

Still, casteism and religious discrimination against specific communities are Nepal's main problems, creating century-long unfairness, inequality and disadvantage over them. Higher castes such as Brahmin, Chhetri and Newar (BCN) have persistently manipulated the rules and regulations to suit their needs, perpetuating their ruling for centuries. They also hold almost all the higher decision-making positions and hardly allow people from other lower castes (Janjatis and Dalits) to enter those powerful governmental offices. As a result, those low-caste communities barely have any say in deciding on the governmental budget, policy and big projects, let alone sharing them. Since they hold all the keys, the higher castes (Nepali elites) decide which door to open and to close at their whim. Doors taking to the other lower-caste communities get shut off all the time, preventing a much-needed lifeline to those already marginalised communities. Such practices have become so common and frustrating that people joked about it in Pokhara, my home town, where most of the Gurungs and other lower-caste communities live. 'Gurungs gather to raise money, and the Bahuns (Brahmins) gather to distribute money', meaning the Gurung community has to do everything by themselves to improve their neighbourhood. In contrast, the Bahun community gets everything done by the government and still has extra money to share. I am not bringing this up to make some community look bad or good, but to show the reality and how crooked the community has become.

The Janjaati (Gurung, Magar, Rai, Limbu, Sherpa, and Tamang) communities might be constrained from governmental, political, intellectual, and institutional opportunities and don't get to share the advantages with them. Still, those communities are primarily unrestricted from other social, cultural and personal choices, and they are doing alright as far as individual families are concerned. The real victims of this feudal caste and religious hierarchy system are the Dalits (Kami, Damai, Sunar, Sarki, and others), whose survival within the community very much depended on the mercy of the higher castes. Nepal has 28 cultural groups of Dalits (untouchables) from different sub-caste groups, such as the hills, the Terai, and the indigenous Dalits of the Newar community in Kathmandu, which are the occupational caste groups possessing unique traditional skills. The Dalits couldn't touch, eat, sit or work together with the higher castes, were forced to live in a shabby makeshift house at the bottom part of the village, and scraped a living working as servants to the higher caste families. A whopping 87 per cent of Dalits don't own any land, whereas the percentage in other communities is just 13 per cent. The Dalits have been treated inhumanely and unfairly discriminated against by the higher caste community for so long that they had no chance of getting out of the ghetto-like hellish life and living a simple and dignified life. As a result, this has created an unmendable division, friction and mistrust among the communities.

Yet, the biggest problem that's crippling Nepal as a country is not having jobs for its youths, and the lack of opportunity within the country is what's forcing them to think for an alternative. Suppose you look back at Nepal's history. In that case, the country was self-sufficient until the 1990s and had various factories such as cement, shoe, garment, cigarette, sugar, tea, and many other household products. Even the Nepal Army had arms and ammunition-making facilities and managed to fulfil its basic needs. Nepal used to import only necessary things while trying to produce the rest within the country. It was the democratic governments that dismantled all of Nepal's young industries, turning today's Nepal with no ambition and too dependent on the outside world. Critics openly alleged India as its mastermind, for they wanted to make Nepal their sole market for Indian products and weak and dependent, too. End of the day, it didn't matter, for whoever was behind it and for whatever reason; they succeeded in their goal. With no industries, Nepal imports almost everything from outside and India has undoubtedly become the principal benefactor.

Nepal's problem, however, continues. With no notable industries, the possibilities of creating jobs are just not there, and the country's youths are paying for this costly mistake. Apart from some jobs in the service and tourism industries, which are mostly restricted to the city areas, the whole country has to rely on agriculture. Even farming hasn't improved much and is still done in the old primitive way. As a result, there are simply no jobs for the country's youths, leaving them only one option: going outside. Today, over six million Nepali youths (one million in India alone) work outside, notably making the workforce supply to foreign countries the only export Nepal has and the country relying on remittance money. A country where there is no value and opportunity for its youths indeed cannot have a bright future in the long term, and one cannot expect much from the leaders of a country that sells its youths, the most precious asset, so cheaply. Nepal has to stop this unfortunate practice at all costs if it aspires to a long and respectful future. Nepali leaders must find a solution to this pressing issue to avoid being condemned by history.

The continuation of the century-long patriarchal society is another fundamental problem in Nepal that hinders the dawning of a fair, equal and balanced society. People still prefer sons to daughters here, and daughters are subject to many unfair and unequal treatments within the community. Although the thinking of new parents is changing in the cities, society still practices prejudices and discrimination against daughters, and its final effects on the community are disastrous. Girls hardly get to study in school, do more chores at home and field, and get married off too early. They also are the most neglected within the family, as many households have more girls than boys. Since daughters don't get any inheritance from the family, they have to rely on their husbands and in-laws for the rest of their lives. They also have to start life from a handicapped and unfavourable position early, forcing them to work doubly harder than the boys usually do. As a result, the country is paying the price for the mistake made by the patriarchal society in Nepal.

They say men and women are like two tyres of a bicycle. One cannot expect a smooth journey without two proper tyres, the same way one cannot expect a happy and prosperous life ahead without men and women. Home is the first school for any child—they say—and a mother plays a crucial role in making a child's life. Children raised by a strong, educated, happy and capable mother will become better people when they grow up. A society where girls and boys get equal treatment and opportunity will have a better future than those without, and the same rule could apply to the country. You don't have to be a rocket scientist to understand Nepal's actual situation in this instance and know in which direction the country is heading. An uneducated mother cannot even help her children with their homework, let alone make them capable people for the country's sake. Regardless of your tradition, belief and faith, treat your daughters the same way you treat your sons and make them capable people. After all, they are your blood and deserve the same equality and opportunity. For the country's sake, everyone in Nepal must get this important lesson into their head and send their sons and daughters to school.

Nepali people must also learn to do their jobs properly, take responsibility for their actions, and protect and preserve their heritage. Nepali people are known for their simple, carefree and fun-loving lifestyle, and they also like joking around. They also drink, gamble and talk a lot. Most importantly, they take almost everything for granted, including life and mostly fail to prepare for a rainy day. Nobody can do all jobs perfectly, for humans are not made of in that way. But everyone can do one job perfectly if he gives his best, and all you need in life is to be good at one job and do it perfectly. To prove this point, one has to look at the status of institutions and facilities provided by foreign countries. Facilities built or set up by foreigners operate smoothly until the foreigners are still around. Things will start to go wrong the moment the foreign supervisors leave the facilities, and it will take just a few years before everything stops to a grounding halt. Due to a lack of proper care and maintenance, the facility cannot continue operation, rendering it useless and eventually abandoned. All foreign-funded projects in Nepal faced the same fate sooner than later, raising a doubtful question about the ability of Nepali people to run a business by themselves. Failing to grasp this life lesson has made many Nepalis insignificant and lost much in life. Nepali people need to learn or care how to do a job properly. Even worse, many don't even know what they want in life, and others don't even bother. As a result, many lives are wasted in vain, ignorance and delusion.

On top of that, Nepali people also believe in parables, myths, witches, superstitions and all kinds of mumbo-jumbos. In the pretext of faith and belief, they also practice various rites and rituals that allow many fakes, cheats and shady characters to thrive in the community. Such useless and unproven practices also create an unnecessary burden for the people, and many have suffered greatly. They also cost money, causing extreme pain and stress among the family members. In some unfortunate cases, they also became the cause of death, putting the immediate family into unbearable pain and emotion. Had they not been so superstitious and backward, they could have avoided so many unnecessary hassles for themselves. Had they been able to differentiate between rights and wrongs, they could have concentrated more on the good things in life by not wasting so much time on those useless and outdated practices.

Another virus ruining the society in Nepal is the lack of a sense of responsibility, and everyone from the top to bottom tiers seems to be affected by this defect. Communities only want to settle everything by talking and waiting to follow up with actions. They also speak in such a sense that they never have to take responsibility for their talking and promise everything, like building a bridge over land without a whiff of shame or guilt. It all starts from the top leaders down to middlemen, and eventually to the general public. As a result, everyone talks, all empty talks, and nothing ever happen at the end. The practice of 'talking only, no action' has become so prevalent that people take it as a professional skill and feel proud of having it.

Nepalis also, meantime, grow fond of another bad habit that's gradually ridding itself of its history and heritage. They need to learn how to preserve their history and lose it so quickly that it will soon become a country without its history. Nepal is known for its magnificent heritage and glorious past. In the Kathmandu valley alone, one can find several historical temples and buildings in every nook and cranny and see how rich historically the country has been. But an expert eye could easily see how old and dilapidated they have become as they have hardly been adequately maintained. The only structures with proper care and maintenance are those protected by UNESCO and receiving foreign funds. Most of the antiques and Gods and Goddesses statues adorned those temples are lost or stolen, and some immoral and greedy Nepalis were complicit in the crime. Nepal hardly has any notable museums, libraries and historic preservation sites. All those ancient scriptures, books and valuable documents were left rotten in old houses as piles of garbage and mostly destroyed by now. They even closed one of the country's top libraries to make room for a hotel, and all those books, documents and papers were found scattered on the construction site as litter. People here in Nepal have no sense of value or understanding about the significance of its history, heritage and legacy, and they hardly preserve them. As a result, only a little of its written history and heritage are left in Nepal.

Whatever remains, even that's biased and selective and doesn't represent the whole community. For instance, Balbhadra Kunwar is revered as a national hero of Nepal, and the story of his bravery is widely read in textbooks. But he was also the first *Lahure* (Gorkha) who served in the Khalsa

Sikh Army of Punjab's Maharaja Ranjit Singh and started the Gorkha legacy. Similarly, whenever people talk about Nepal's democracy, they always talk about BP Koirala, Sukra Raj Shastri, Dashrath Chand, and Ganga Lal Shrestha. But several other individuals had contributed a great deal that still needed to be mentioned in Nepal's textbooks and history books. Gyan Bahadur Yakthumba (1920-1970) was one such big name whose contribution to Nepal was exceptional. Starting as a member of the Nepali Congress in Kolkata, he formed the Janamukti Sena (Freedom Fighters) with other Gorkha veterans. He waged the armed revolution against the Rana oligarchy as one of its leading commanders. They fought many successful battles against the Nepal Army, notably in Birgunj, Biratnagar, Uppardang Ghadi, and other parts of eastern Nepal. Eventually, they helped end the 105-year-old Rana's autocratic regime. After serving as the Baddahakim of Ilam in the east of Nepal, he returned to Kathmandu as DIG (Deputy Inspector General) of Nepal Police. Then he served as the IGP (Inspector General of Police) until 1960, when King Mahendra ended Nepal's first democratic system and imprisoned all leaders, including him. Gyan Bahadur Yakthumba, a democratic fighter, charismatic and far-sighted leader, and wise and witty patriot, played a massive role in forming the modern-day Nepal Police Force and ended his remarkable life as an ambassador of Nepal. And yet, sadly, the country and its people have failed to recognise him and his contributions.

All in all, Nepalis themselves are solely responsible for their current situation. A country surviving on remittance money from its youths working as cheap labour in foreign countries must also learn to respect their contributions. Nepal has India on its three sides and the Himalayas on the north—making Nepal geographically handicapped and entirely reliant on India. One can come up with a hell of an argument on this topic, but whether to make it an excuse or deal with it right away, the choice must be Nepali people alone. With similarities in language, religion, tradition, culture, and way of life, unsurprisingly, both Nepal and India have a long and robust relationship as neighbours. Yet, geography is the main reason. Not to mention that Nepal's political leaders are bred and groomed in India, and they could hardly think beyond New Delhi. And undoubtedly, India wields tremendous power and influence over Nepal. Yet, blaming India for Nepal's situation is like blaming your neighbours for your problems, which is cowardly and wrong. The shortcoming is within you; either you accept it or start doing something about it. The choice is always yours.

Foreign donors have made Nepal a testing ground, and the Nepali people lab animals. If they want to stop being guinea pigs, they must stop talking and start working. Nepal is blessed with abundant natural beauty and resources; all they have to do is look around. They don't have to do many things at once but do one thing at a time and correctly. Many people already know that Nepal is one of the wealthiest countries in the world in natural water, and water can be the silver bullet that can kill all the diseases that Nepal is suffering from. In the modern age of global warming and renewable energy, going electric is eco-friendly and the best option and Nepal have plenty of water to make that dream a reality. Nepal should start a nationwide project of producing electricity through all of its rivers within Nepal. Start using electricity at home, work, and everywhere, including household products, office items, factory machines, electric vehicles on the road, and whatever extra electricity it could produce, export to other countries like India and Bangladesh. If executed properly, this could make Nepal a confident and self-reliant nation, if not rich. Most importantly, they will never have to worry about the Indian blockade and experience the same humiliation again.

There are better options than surviving on remittance money alone for Nepal. It's like keeping a sick person alive by giving him oxygen. The oxygen won't cure him, and he will collapse when the oxygen dries up. The time for all the Nepali people to speak up arrived now, for it's the decision-making time for the whole nation. Either you accept the current situation and live on as a vassal nation, or do something to improve the situation and live with dignity and honour. The decision is always yours; whatever it is, be brave enough to own it.

The Chief Architects of the Gorkha Grief

'You come to my house each year; I welcome you as my friend; you take my best sons, train them as soldiers, make them fight your dirty war, and send them back to us when they are old and weak. And you have been doing it for the last 207 years, yet I haven't said a word against it.' One can be excused for thinking of it as a myth or taken straight from a page of fiction. But unfortunately, this is not a myth but a reality, and that's precisely what the British have continuously been doing to Nepal from 1815 to the present day. Despite never being a British colony, how did Nepal ended up in such a humiliating, anarchical and pathetic position? One must delve a little bit more into its background history and the Nepali way of doing things in general to understand this sad story.

The social, cultural, financial, political, and communal implications of the Gorkha institution on Nepal were massive, and the country has still not recovered from the impact yet even today. Nepal is still a poor, underdeveloped, and weak government; the Gorkha institution is one of the main reasons Nepal got into this situation. The British must bear some blame as the chief architect of this Gorkha grief. And yet, the saddest part of this sorry saga is that Nepal still treats the British as its best friend and never dares to point a finger at them.

The first time the British met with the Gorkhas was in 1767 when a team of 2,400 men came to Nepal on the request of the then Newari King Jaya Prakash Malla was ambushed at Sindhuli Gadhi, and suffered a humiliating defeat at the hand of the ragtag Gorkhali Army, later known as the 'Kinloch Expedition'. As the British extended their grip on power throughout India, they still remembered the humiliating defeat and the mysterious and exotic place called Nepal. They also wanted to have a share of Nepal's copper and silver minting, and a trade route to Tibet's gold mining, which eventually led to a decisive war between the two powers in 1814. This was known as the Anglo-Gorkha War of 1814-16, in which the British ultimately won and crushed the Gorkha's aspirations once and for all as a regional power. The British also achieved three main goals from the war: Opened a trade route to Tibet, turned Nepal into a vassal country by establishing British residency in Kathmandu, and made Nepal a toothless tiger by enlisting the Gorkhas in the British Indian Army. This was done so Nepal could never pose any danger to its hegemonies power in India. Besides this, the British also took away all the lands Nepal had won so far and clipped its wing through the signing of the Sugauli Treaty in 1816. Nepal has geographically remained more or less the same size today as it was by then, but the ripple effect caused by the treaty are felt as hard today as they had been in 1816.

If there was any race of people that understood the Nepalis better than they understood themselves, it was the British. They knew Nepal was poor, and they knew Nepalis were desperate. Most importantly, they knew the Nepalis' mercenary nature as a weakness that could be exploited to the maximum for their benefit. With that shrewdness alone, they understood precisely how the Nepalis should be treated and the British were handsomely rewarded as a result. After stripping Nepal of any potential danger, the British started a carefully thought-out two-prong strategy to keep Nepal weak and dependent, so it would never threaten their supremacy in India. They operated through the military, by enlisting the

Gorkhas in the British Indian Army, and also enforced their authority through civilization migration, by encouraging mass civilian migration to those newly acquired territories within India. The policy worked so brilliantly that it became one of the foundations of their rule in India and helped achieve both goals they had set out with. The merciless exploitations of simple people like the Gorkhas was the backbone of British rule in India. They helped achieve tremendous successes that wouldn't have been possible without the Gorkhas on their side. The British might have gone a long time ago, but its implications on those poor Gorkhas are as natural and painful as they had been before. History might favour the winning side, but we are here to highlight Gorkha's plights.

Once the British secured the services of the loyal, brave, and obedient Gorkhas, they started the campaign of conquering India in earnest. First was the Pindaris, followed by Jats, Marathas, and Sikhs, and then the tribal people of Northwest and Northeast India. They also fought several times with the Burmese and Afghanistanis and contributed massively to the making of modern India. There wasn't a single war in which the Gorkhas didn't fight for the British cause and they helped continue the British rule in India for so long. In other words, it won't be an exaggeration to state that the British government in India would not have been possible without the Gorkhas.

While their cousins fought with the tribal militiamen on the hills of the Northwest frontiers, the second phase of the master plan was well underway east of Nepal and mass migrations of Nepali people ensued. As the British captured more territories in the North East, they found more empty lands, thick jungles, inhabitable hills, ravines and swamps full of wild plants and animals. They needed people with sturdy hands, a frugal lifestyle, and willpower to overcome any austerity. They needed farmers who could clear the jungle and weeds, till the land, and create beautiful terraces. They needed cow herders with massive numbers of animals that could graze the empty grassland and provide enough milk and manure as a lifeline. They constructed roads, and labourers were required. They brought railways and needed more railway workers. They found oil and coal mines, and miners were required to extract them from the ground. They found tea and needed enough hands to pick those money-making green tea leaves. With nothing but an able body, simple mind, and willingness to do anything to survive, the Gorkhas were the readymade solution for all the British problems in India. The British never shied away from taking full advantage of the poor Gorkhas for the next two centuries.

In both the First and Second World Wars, as if fighting in the Indian subcontinent was not enough, the British didn't hesitate to send the Gorkha soldiers outside India to fight their dirty wars. Nepali leaders didn't leave a stone unturned in supporting the British and let opened all the doors. The whole of Nepal was there for the British to use. The first battle came in the shape of a horrendous sea voyage, as the Gorkhas, who came from a landlocked country like Nepal, had no experience of a sea voyage before, and many had suffered greatly. They didn't hide from their responsibility as soldiers and fought in the chilling cold of Europe, the scorching heat of Africa, and the dried sand of the Middle East. Others performed their duty in the thick jungle of Burma, Malaysia, and Borneo. Many perished in the line of duty, fighting a war that, in reality, was not their own, leaving their loved ones back home in anguish with no way to know how they had died and where they were buried. And yet, not even a whiff of complaint was ever heard from the Gorkhas.

As the British advanced further into the hostile tribal land of Northeast India, they found more scarcely occupied vast lands, creating another headache for them. The administrative staff consisted of some military personnel. Christian missionaries were in small numbers and faced raids from the tribal outfits, making it a state concern that needed a permanent fix. To improve staff safety and protect the state's property, the British rehired those retired Gorkhas as watchmen, house servants, drivers, or gardeners at their colonies, encouraging them to stay behind after they retired from the regular services. The British eventually made it a long-term policy and allowed Gorkha colonies in those remote places. Those Gorkha colonies would subsequently grow into thriving Gorkha villages and served the purposes very well for which they established—security and sovereignty. Having Gorkha villages alongside the border served two primary goals for the British. Firstly, they drew young blood needed for the military services from the community, and secondly, having a village or residence of your people in the border areas proved your sovereignty over the scarcely marked bordering lands. We still find Gorkha villages in those remote border areas of Northeast states like Arunachal Pradesh, Nagaland, and Manipur. They were planted there by the British and served a purpose.

After India's independence in 1947, the British and India divided the then country's most precious asset, the British Indian Gorkha Brigade, between them. To appease Prime Minister Nehru's unwillingness, the British had to offer the Andaman and Nicobar Islands to India in exchange for the Gorkhas. Finally, four out of ten regiments followed the British to Malaya (currently Malaysia and Singapore) while the remaining six stayed behind. During their time in Southeast Asia, the Gorkhas fought two lengthy and costly battles—first, dealing with the Communist insurgency, also known as the Malay Emergency 1948-60, and second, the Borneo Confrontation 1963-66 with Indonesian troops. Almost three hundred Gorkhas lost their lives, and many more were injured.

As the number of British colonies decreased, so did the Gorkhas' numbers in the Brigade. When Malaysia and Singapore gained independence, and the Gorkha Brigade moved to Hong Kong in 1971, almost half of the Gorkhas were dismissed from the services. Similarly, two third of the total force lost their job before 1997, when Hong Kong, the last British colony in Asia, returned to China. Once the British lost all their colonies, they didn't see the usefulness of the Gorkhas, and only a token of the Gorkha Brigade existed in the UK. About 3,500 Gorkhas are currently serving in the British Army and continuing the legacy that's over 207 years old. Apart from the Brigade of Gorkhas in the UK, 2000 Gorkhas also serve in the Singapore Police and another 500 men in the Gorkha Reserve Unit (GRU) Brunei.

On the request of the Sultan of Brunei, the British have also been lending out one Gorkha Infantry Battalion to Brunei and working as Brunei's security force since 1962. Similarly, the British also help conduct the recruiting and other training requirements for the Singapore Police in Nepal. The British received a substantial amount of money for the services provided, and the funds received from these two nations (Singapore and Brunei) for trading the Gorkha's services off to them is likely more than enough to pay for the expenses of the Gorkha Brigade in the UK. In other words, the Gorkhas are paying for their own services and technically costing the British government nothing—a typical example of British shrewdness and business acumen.

If you look at it from the outside, you won't see any problem. Both Singapore and Brunei have been British colonies and the current arrangements predates them. But if you see it from its current and international position, one could easily find a big problem. One must remember that Singapore and Brunei are not British colonies but sovereign countries in their own right. As required by international laws, there should have been an agreement between the British, Singapore, and Brunei, in consultation with Nepal, before such practices could commence. The treaty that enlists the Gorkha's services to the British Army doesn't have a provision for such a third-party arrangement, thus, making the British's unilateral practice illegal. Unless such mistakes are rectified through a newly reviewed treaty between concerned countries, including Nepal, the practice can be taken as a case of human trafficking and reported to the human rights court for the immediate cessation of the practice and demand for compensation.

I wouldn't hold my breath in anticipation of it just yet, however. Of course, the chance of this happening to the British is almost zero to none, as Nepali elites care more about donation money than the dignity and well-being of its people. The British also know how to shut off the mouths of the Nepali elite. Every time they made a big decision, such as the 1969 and 1994 rundowns when more than half of the Gorkhas lost their job, the British sent over a big name to leader, and left them with some form of an explanation. Since the Nepali elites have always had a weak knee for the British, the oppressors have never had to sweat for anything, always getting what they want. Nepali elites genuinely feel privileged to be friended by the British and have thus never haggled with the British for anything for the country. As a result, Nepal has always needed to catch up in this lopsided relationship between the two countries.

If the British can get away with the shameful and continuous exploitation of the Gorkhas for 207 years, there is no reason for them to consider stopping now. The ongoing Gorkha exploitations are not only limited to the government level but also extended to the individual. Former British officers have significantly benefited by offering the services of ex-Gorkha members to international security firms working in dangerous and war-torn countries such as Iraq, the Gulf Nations, Africa, and Afghanistan. They also collaborated with Gorkha officers to open human resources agencies that offer security support, bodyguard details, and other services to rich and famous corporations in Hong Kong, Brunei, and other wealthy countries. In the name of providing opportunities and helping ex-Gorkha servicemen, these British officers earned big money with the labours of the Gorkhas, and such practices will continue in the future.

The British still come to Nepal once a year, select 150-300 youths and take them to the UK to help continue the Gorkha legacy. The saddest thing is not the fact that more than 20-30 thousand youths compete for these limited positions, allowing the British to select the best of the bests from the country. The saddest thing is there are no alternatives for the country's youths, and they all have to scrape for leftovers provided by the outsiders that are disguised as an opportunity. The country's so-called elites do not care enough to raise an eyebrow at this, let alone do anything to stop it.

The British used flattery, trickery, and treachery to prolong the one-sided Anglo-Nepal relationship for as long as possible, and the Gorkhas were/are the main factor behind all this. They genuinely made the Nepali elites believe the British were Nepal's real friends, but it was lip service. Whenever they received a massive contribution from Nepal, such as the supply of over a quarter of a million Gorkhas in WW2, in flattery, they showered the Nepali leaders with several British honorary medals and awards such as Grand Cross of the Bath, Knights Grand Commander of the Order of the Indian Empire, Grand Commander of the Order of the Star of India, Grand Cross of the Order of St. Michael and St. George, and the Imperial Order of Par Excellence, etc. The British awarded those awards to the Nepali leaders as this did not cost them anything.

The Tripartite Treaty of 1947, signed by Nepal, the United Kingdom, and India that is still the primary basis on which the Gorkhas are serving in by the British and Indian armies, was conducted in a rather dubious situation. The treaty papers signed by both British and India differed from those signed by Nepal. The reason behind this was the inclusion of a separate term called the IPC (Indian Pay Code) that also applied to the British Gorkhas throughout their services in Asia from 1948 to 1994. The Nepali side was neither consulted nor informed on this issue, and the ignorant Nepali leaders have yet to show interest in this matter. The explanation given for this trickery was to bring the British Gorkha's pay on par with their counterparts in India, but the main reason was the British penchant for exploitation. They wanted to pay the Gorkhas as little as they could as they were accustomed to having the Gorkhas cheap. The British paid the Gorkhas even lesser than the Philipino maids in Hong Kong and had to adjust adjust the Gorkhas' salaries after the Hong Kong government introduced new legislation on minimum wages in the late eighties. This was why the Gorkhas have been fighting for equality for the last thirty-two years and the flagrant British policy of trading the Gorkhas off to a third country like Singapore and Brunei, as described above, is nothing less than a sign of betrayal for which they should be shamed and condemned by the international community.

As if the Gorkhas' enlistment in their regular Army for over 207 years was not enough, the senior British officers also used the Gorkha veterans to make more money. By charging exorbitant prices to their clients and paying a pittance to the Gorkhas, they made a vast fortune out of the blood, sweat, and tears of the naive Gorkhas and continued exploiting them.

It has been decades, if not centuries since the British have more or less left India, but their decisions' repercussions still haunt the Nepali people even today. India, the country that has inherited the new nation, also inherited its old master's tricks and treacheries and willingly used them against its poor and small neighbours. It has been just a change of the master at the very top, the rest remains the same as before, and the unfair treatment, exploitation and bullying continues. The British were the main reason for Nepal's current situation, too weak, poor and too dependent. Nepal never got to start anything on its own, never learned to walk and run and be able to stand on its own feet. In return for Nepal's friendship, they gave Nepal betrayal and misery. In return for the Nepali people's sacrifices, they rewarded Nepal with a fake smile, false hope, and a ruined country. In brief, Nepal is where it is today mainly because of the British and the British must take moral responsibility for its wrongdoing—this is the least they could do, acknowledging their not-so-gracious role in the past. This debt of honour is what the British owe to its Gorkhas, and the Nepali people, especially the youth, should never forget that. They shouldn't hold on to it with regret, remorse, or revenge in mind, but only as a history lesson that shows that such injustice, exploitation, and the unfair treatment of people should never be repeated.

The Position of the Nepali Elites

People always get the leaders they deserve they say, but as far as Nepalis are concerned, I assume that's quite unfair. Despite all their weaknesses, naiveties, and shortcomings, Nepali people deserve much better leaders than the ones they have had. Successful people don't blame luck or others. Instead, they start working hard and becoming wise. Still, I believe that luck plays a crucial part in our lives, and God has been a little bit harsh to the Nepalis in this department. As the old saying goes, history never lies, and we might have to invoke some of our past histories to prove this point.

After King Prithvi Narayan Shah, the founding father of Nepal, almost all of his descendants turned out to be weak and uninspiring rulers. One was eccentric, and the others were too young and inexperienced. As a result, Nepal was ruled by a group of regents such as the queens, mothers, prime ministers, the King's uncle, and an army chief before strong man Jang Bahadur Rana took over the power and established the Rana oligarchy that lasted for the next 105 years. They kept the nation in the dark by banning schools, stopping developments, and plunging it further into poverty. While the public suffered in sheer misery, they indulged in the high life, looted the nation's assets, and forced the people down the drain. As if life was not already hard enough, the cruel Rana regime levied a higher tax on the poor to support their luxurious lifestyle, forcing helpless farmers to migrate eastward in search of better farming land.

To give legitimacy and continuity to their rule, Bir Shamsher officially sanctioned the Gorkha's enlistment into the British Indian Army in 1886. He helped make that practice one of Nepal's traditions still going on strong today. Chandra Shamsher took it to the next level and sent over 200,000 Gorkhas to fight for the British in WW1 alone. One in ten never returned home, whereas ten of thousands returned with broken arms and legs and damaged heads. Not to be outdone, Juddha Shamsher opened up the whole of Nepal for the British, including the national treasury, sent out a quarter of a million Gorkhas out of the six million population to fight for the British in WW2 where 33,000 men died, and tens of thousands were injured. Despite not being a member country of the warring side, Nepal suffered one of the heaviest casualties in both WW1 and WW2, which baffled many and raised questions about the sanity of Nepali leaders. Was it worth sacrificing so many lives?

The cruel autocratic Rana regime ended in 1951. Still, Mohan Shamsher, the last Prime Minister of the Rana oligarchy, made one previous treaty with the newly independent India, and Nepali people from both sides of the border are still experiencing its chilling effects even today. After the demise of the Rana regime, democracy prevailed in Nepal for good. But the jubilation didn't last too long as King Mahendra killed it prematurely by introducing a new system called the Panchayati. Mahendra was the one from the Shah dynasty who acted like a real king and promoted actual developments in Nepal. He died a bit too early, and his son, King Birendra, the most beloved King of Nepal, willingly decided to become a constitutional king in 1990 to allow a multi-party system as demanded by the aspirations of the Nepali people.

Despite Nepal having a multi-party system and a constitutional king, the Maoist insurgency ravaged the country with internal fighting, killing, and displacement of many people, further leading the nation to poverty. The killing of King Birendra and his entire family in 2001 brought the country to almost a halt. The accession of his unpopular brother King Gyanendra to the throne didn't help, and the brutal Maoist insurgency further tore the country apart. After 240 years of its rule, the monarchy ended in Nepal in 2008 when the King finally relented and paved the way for establishing the new Federal Democratic Republic of Nepal. With its first constitution introduced in 2015, everyone took a sigh of relief and hoped for the best.

Unfortunately, not much has changed since then, and the Nepali people's aspirations for good governance, improvement in their livelihood, and development at the local, provincial, and eventually national levels didn't materialise. The leaders they had chosen to lead the country turned out to be more corrupt, unreliable, incapable, greedy, selfish, and dishonest than those before and expecting this shameless bunches to end the country's miseries was the last thing they could have hoped. A statement like 'the whole nation was hugely disappointed' would have been an understatement—the whole nation was shattered.

The Nepali rulers had always been selfish, short-sighted, narrow-minded, self-enriching, cruel, erratic, corrupted, greedy, and irresponsible throughout their history. Whether during the Rana Regime or the post-Rana Regime, everything they did was to prolong their own rule and power, and they did almost nothing for the country but enrich themselves. The country's current situation has become so fragile and weakened over time that it could be divided into two groups: the ruling elites and the rest. To understand these two groups, one must know a brief history of the Nepali people. They were divided into two main groups, the people from the north (Mongoloids) and the south (Indo-Aryans) at different periods of history. Both groups have various tribes, castes, and sub-castes among them, and their current position within the country was determined by one sole factor—the Gorkha institution.

The Nepali political leaders also suffer from another incurable disease that shows how lowly, callous, and undeserving hypocrites they are and how they lie in front of your face without blinking their eyes. This charade has been going on for decades, making a fool of the public repeatedly. They all sound good when they stand as the opposition party—they say all the right words, and present themselves as a new saviour. Being cheated and betrayed for decades, the desperate public see a new hope and start pouring all their hopes, aspirations, and expectation of the future into the new guy. Even a tiny semblance of goodness looks magical; the hopeless public finds a new messiah and starts worshipping him like a God. They do all this only to be disappointed again, for the leader inevitably shows his true face when he is in power and starts behaving like the same old farts e.g., plundering the nation's assets with both hands as if it was his fiefdom. Nepal must be one of the unluckiest countries in the world, where all those unfit, undeserving, and mediocre people fill all the critical and decision-making positions. Even worse, the public always falls for those leaders' silky words and gets betrayed repeatedly. But as the old saying goes—one cannot make a clap with one hand alone, and the public must take half the blame for their position. If you, as a member of the people, don't know the value of your voting right and sell it out for a dime (a meal with meat popular among the public), you have no one but yourself to blame for all the suffering.

Since the Gorkha institution started in 1815 and the British favoured the Mongoloid community out of the two; the Indo-Aryan community had no option but to stay behind and dig in their heels. Over the two centuries, they have occupied almost every governmental, civilian, and commercial position and established themselves as the country's elites. The Gorkha community, which stayed outside the country most of the time, lost out in the long term and ended up playing second fiddle to the ruling elites. The Nepali elites certainly have social, financial, and political motives for not letting the Gorkha community come near their power base; hence, neglecting and downplaying the Gorkha's glory would benefit their cause of keeping the power for themselves. As a result, the Gorkhas lost out in this internal game and the community never recovered.

To the Nepali elites, the Gorkhas were the troublemakers from early on that they could have done without. Therefore, they were more than willing to pawn them for their ulterior motives when the British came in for the Gorkhas. Initially, one Gorkha was sold for one rifle by the Ranas. Before long, the Gorkha institution became a precious asset they could exchange for power, money, and even the country's sovereignty, and the Ranas used them to their maximum benefit. In brief, the Gorkha institution was the factor that kept the Ranas in power for so long and only ended when the British departed from India. On their way out, the Ranas signed a treaty with India that clipped most of Nepal's future aspirations and developments as a country. Nepalis are still suffering from the repercussions today, seven decades later.

It has been over seventy-one years since the dark days of Rana's regime ended. Nepal has gone through many upheavals since then, so much so that they even managed to get rid of the 240-year-old monarchy among them. Yet, one thing has remained the same for centuries—the way Nepali elites behave. If the Ranas did it openly, the modern Nepali elites would do it behind the door, making it more harmful and dangerous to the country.

The Ranas did only make the Gorkhas a *Lahure* ccommunity; the new elites have made the entire Nepali communities new *Lahures* as they forced Nepali youths to any willing nations that would accept them as cheap labour. Within the last seven decades, the Nepali elites have managed to sell out all of its rivers and water resources to India while the country is still working to solve its electricity shortage problem. All the factories King Mahendra had managed to assemble in his short tenure have all closed down. Institutions like education, health, public transportation, finance and banking, insurance, and IT (information technology) have been commercialised and outsourced. Army factories making arms and ammunition have been closed down, and all the fitted machines were sold to foreigners as scrap metals. The nation doesn't even have a single research and innovation centre, as it relies solely on the data provided by foreign institutions. The country has yet to learn what natural resources and mines are found within Nepal, and all of its wild plants and herbals are controlled by foreign pharmaceutical firms. Foreign visitors come to Nepal simply because the Himalayas are there, but the country has yet to do anything to improve the tourism industry except charge mountain climbing fees. Everything they used to make in Nepal has all ceased. Even a relic of an old factory no longer exists, making one feel like the whole country has stopped trying.

The country has become so dependent on the outside world that almost everything they need in Nepal has to come from outside, so much so that it can't even provide enough fertiliser to its farmers today. Not a single project is done without foreign involvement. Kathmandu Valley is full of people from foreign embassies, INGOs, and other institutions with involvements in such sectors as education, health, politics, social, religion, media, community improvement, IT, climate, human rights, gender and race equality, and so on, and one can hardly find a person of position and power who has no affiliation with any one of those foreigners. Seeing those foreigners so active and openly involved in Nepal, one could be easily forgiven for questioning their role in Nepal's internal affairs. Nepali elites are solely responsible for the country's current situation. These elites have weak knees for the foreign powers and suffer from an inferior complexity and a servility attitude disorder. Their actions in front of foreign powers have often proven that they have disgraced the nation and the people. Even a mid-sized Dharmaguru with a dubious character and reputation from India could call upon all the prominent leaders of Nepali politics. One of the Nepali national leaders got a lousy name for endorsing a controversial Christian church leader from Korea and their campaign in Nepal.

Similarly, the usual scenes of Nepali elites lining up at the Indian embassy whenever the new ambassador arrives or ends his time in Nepal are nothing new to Nepali people. Nepali elites are notoriously renowned for their shameless, spineless, and disgraceful sycophancy in front of foreign powers like India, the US, the British, and Europe. They would do anything to hang on to power.

The Nepali elites have made the country poor, weak, and too dependent on outside countries and turned it into a mere skeleton with no jobs, hope, or future for its youths. The country's youths have no choice but to leave and work as cheap labours in foreign countries where they get used, mistreated and exploited under inhumane conditions. Nepal survives on remittance money sent home from those workers as it makes up over 40 per cent of its economy. Many are killed in Gulf nations, beaten up as cattle in Malaysia, and sold as enslaved people and prostitutes in India. Yet, Nepali elites who are supposed to take care of their citizens do nothing to protect them. Instead of helping them, some Nepali embassy staff harass and extort money from these poor youths. Others are in cahoots with unscrupulous foreign agencies to milk those poor and naïve Nepali youths. The way the greedy customs officials prey on those returning home at the Kathmandu airport is a national disgrace.

Bureaucracy is so ripe that nothing happens without a bribe. Political parties have infiltrated almost every governmental and private department, and nobody can survive without a party affiliation. Compared to other developed nations where government officials are there to serve the public, here in Nepal, it is the opposite, and a job can only be done by pleasing the government officials. They are greedy, rude, and corrupt and act like thugs with impunity and a zero sense of responsibility. Worst of them all, none of the Nepali elites work like they represent the public, show no regard for the reputation and prestige of the country and its people, and behave arbitrarily like an individual of their own. They don't care about the consequences of their actions or the effects they might have on the country and its people—they do whatever they want. Their efforts are primarily based on their personal and party benefits; thus, the country is the last thing they have on their minds.

Nepal is a beautiful country surrounded by the majestic Himalayas, beautiful serene mountains, and lush green natural sceneries. It's also blessed with abundant natural resources, beautiful rivers, and a clean, soothing climate. Yet, its biggest asset is its people of various races, cultures, traditions, and simplicity. With a little bit of intelligence, diligence, and a sense of belonging and responsibility, Nepal could have been one of the best countries, if not the riches and most powerful, in the world. It was blessed by such an abundance of natural resources as gifts, it could have been not hard at all. But look what it had become. Poor, weak, and too dependent on the outside world—one could hardly believe what had transpired. It morphed into a beggar with a golden bowl in a few decades, and it has all but to blame itself for its current situation. Outside forces have played a massive role in making Nepal what it is today, but blaming others alone won't take away all the mistakes it made as a country. The people of the country alone are responsible for making or breaking the country they belong to, and the Nepali people are no exception.

People might hate me for badmouthing Nepal, but one must understand that someone has to confront the truth, and if by speaking the truth helps my motherland, I am ready to accept the consequences. One doesn't have to look too far back to realise how low Nepal has sunk in the last few decades and how it has lost its glitter on the international stage. There were days when powerful countries like the US, the UK, and others used to welcome Nepali leaders with a massive display of pomps, pageantries, and gun salutes. Heads of state like the kings, queens, presidents, and prime ministers would line up with their wives and husbands at the airport to personally receive the Nepali leaders and the news of their visit used to make headlines in national papers of the country. During King Mahendra's coronation alone, over four hundred state guests attended the proceeding. Over 160 foreign media correspondents came to Kathmandu representing news outlets worldwide, including the New York Times. Nowadays, whenever Nepali state leaders visit a foreign country, the only individuals that welcome them are junior members of the foreign ministry of the host nation, staff from the Nepali embassy, and some gadflies from the Nepali diaspora communities. Not a single media outlet of the host nation writes anything about the visit. This is the reality of today's Nepal. In a matter of decades, it has turned into a pauper nation from one of the world's most respectable and admired countries, and one might wonder how this is even possible. But look no further, as you all know where the problem lies.

Nepali elites must take all the blames for what they have done to the country and its people. It's also true that Nepal needed a better leader, too. But they were your leaders. Whether you got to choose them or not, it was your leader. It was not of your making that they turned out so immoral, selfish, and greedy. But you were the ones who accepted them, let them run over you, and you watched on as they plundered the country. It is unfortunate that they were Nepalis. But as people of the country, it was your responsibility too. After all, it was your country, life, and society. If you don't take care of it, who will then? Please ask yourself at least once. Please keep that in mind, and you will know the correct answer. Once every Nepali finds that answer, everything will turn our alright, and Nepal will never have to suffer the same fate and indignity that it has again.

✯ ✯ ✯

How Does Nepal View India?

As we approached the border crossing in west Nepal, I noticed two things that captured my attention—the Indian border checkpoint and the barrage on the Mahakali River. The Nepali checkpoint was pretty simple and was a checkpoint only in the name. In contrast, the Indian one was big, manned by several armed security personnel, and located far inside Nepali territory. The barrage on the Mahakali River had only one water canal, and water from the river flowed only one side towards India. Similarly, Indian airlines also conduct their separate security checkup in Kathmandu airport after passengers have gone through all security procedures in Nepal. One doesn't have to be a genius to see the problem here, and such a lopsided practice like this one is the reason that shapes Nepal's views about India, and they have not always been favourable.

The end of British rule in India also paved the way for Rana's demise in Nepal. The Indians inherited a new nation and their colonial master's big-brother mentality. Mohan Shamsher, the last Rana Prime Minister of Nepal, seemed more than willing to appease the new master in Delhi. To prolong and safeguard Rana's autocratic rule in Nepal, he hurriedly signed the India-Nepal Peace Treaty of 1950, making Nepal India's vassal nation since then. Swiped under the tide of the time, the Ranas couldn't save themselves and had to accept the change. In this regard, Indians were nothing like the British and saw no values hanging onto an outdated and autocratic ruler like the Ranas. The Ranas might have gone for good, but the treaty remains, and the entire country still suffers its repercussions today.

The treaty's signing immediately brought Nepal under India's security umbrella, giving India the much sought-after access and use of Nepal's territories for security purposes. Perceived as the main threat by the US, they wanted to use Nepal as a buffer zone between Communist China and democratic India. The Indian military was mobilised to build roads, buildings, and other significant facilities within Nepal. The Indian Army also built and manned seventeen army outposts alongside the Himalayan region on China border. Since Nepal had no air force or strong Army in the 1950s, both the air and ground of Nepal became a thumping place for the Indian army boots. Nepal also wasn't allowed to buy arms or ammunition from a third country without India's permission. India agreed to withdraw all (except one at Lipulekh) military outposts from the northern frontier during King Mahendra's tenure in 1969.

India's old policy of interfering in Nepal's internal affairs is nothing new, and this must be the only topic on which all Nepalis agree. The Indian embassy staffs get pretty active during the election. News about Indian agencies being caught with a van full of fake voting papers and suitcases full of cash exchanging hands between political leaders is pretty standard. It's also a common belief in Nepal that leaders can only hold on to power with New Delhi's blessing, and India never leaves a stone unturned in having their men in power. Besides, all of the political leaders from Nepal were/are educated and learned their trade in India, and they hardly see beyond New Delhi. Some of Nepal's top leaders are alleged to have political connections with the corridor of powers in New Delhi. They are suspected of doing India's bidding to hang on to power, and India does nothing on its part to quell such allegations.

Still, it's not India's perpetual interference in Nepal's affairs that Nepali people hate, for they could do almost nothing about it anyway. But it's the shameless and spineless Nepali leaders and their selfish, suspicious and submissive character that Nepali people loathe the most. Until New Delhi improves its attitude towards Nepal, no patriotic Nepalis could accept the situation and start liking India for good.

The other issue that touched Nepali people's nerves is India's ongoing pursuit of capturing Nepal's rivers at all costs. It has acquired the right to develop almost all of Nepal's major rivers. When I visited the Koshi barrage in 2018, I was surprised to hear that the Indians held the keys to the operation. Once the barrage was closed, the flooding areas on Nepal's side were huge, and the damages sustained by the farmers were substantial. Since the Indian side controls the barrage, they close it in the rainy season and open it in the winter, causing a double-whammy for the Nepal side. They get over-flooded in the summer and face a dry season in the winter, creating plenty of problems for the farmers that could have been avoided had the Indian side been a bit fairer. These are genuine grievances from real people whose livelihoods have been adversely affected by the barrage, and I genuinely felt for those poor individuals. What's more, that was just one of the many examples the general people were facing within Nepal, and such unfair practices are not doing any good for India's image.

India also has a monopoly on Nepal's other natural resources and gets its raw materials from Nepal. Nepali herbs, weeds, and other plants of medicinal value fulfil the demands of India's pharmaceutical and Ayurvedic companies, and they get it almost for free. When they wrap it in a capsule and send it back to Nepal, poor Nepalis have to pay a fortune to get their medicines, and they still don't get it enough when they need it the most. In other words, Nepal has everything that nature has to offer. The Nepalis require more skill and knowledge to turn them into medicine but instead end up paying over a hundred times more to get it. Knowledge is everything. If you don't have it or don't put effort into getting it, you get preyed upon by other, more intelligent people or countries. Still, India's absorption of Nepal's natural resources gives Nepali people another reason for resenting the Indians, and the frustration will only grow over time.

Another issue that irritates most Nepalis is India's tendency to own every mythical and religious figures, such as Mother Sita and Lord Buddha, as their own on the international stage, ensuing heated debates between nationalists and followers from both sides. Some Indian Hindu extremists (Shivbhakts—Lord Shiva's devotees) also have the audacity of claiming the Kailash Parbat (the Himalayas) as their own, due to their belief that it remains Lord Shiva's residence. India also wants Nepal to be as submissive and dependent as Bhutan, and expresses displeasure with Nepal's close ties with China. There shouldn't be any comparisons between Nepal and Bhutan, for they are two countries distinct in size, population, and the diversity of its people. India should be more sensitive and careful about Nepal's religious, political, and emotional feelings.

The continuation of Gorkha's enlistment in the Indian Army is another reason that creates an unbalanced relationship between the two countries. Having learned everything from their old colonial master, the British, India takes it as a master-servant relationship and acts like they are doing a favour to Nepal. On the contrary, the Gorkhas perceives this as a tradition. Since they have been loyal, honourable, and committed to their duties, they shouldn't have to beg for it and hate India's condescending behaviour and taken-for-granted approaches. Furthermore, India has also accused China of wanting to enlist the Gorkhas in their Army. Even so, it should be a matter that remains between Nepal and China, for India doesn't have a monopoly on the Gorkha's enlistment; Nepal should be the one to make decisions about its people, including the Gorkhas. India should be more considerate and respectful towards, if not Nepal, but at least the Gorkhas who have sacrificed their lives for India over the last two centuries.

The most controversial issue of the Nepal-India Treaty of 1950 is the open border policy that allows people from both sides to visit, work, buy property and run a business in both countries, enabling millions of people from both countries to live across the border. People of Nepali origin crossed the border for a better life as they were simple people; economic migrants looking for a better livelihood. In contrast, people of Indian origin came to Nepal with a goal. They aimed to be a majority in Terai through demography. The entire plains of Terai were scarcely populated before the 1950s, mainly occupied by the Tharus and other indigenous communities, primarily those neglected by the rulers from Kathmandu. The people from the hills came down to eradicate deadly malaria in the mid-1950s. The introduction of King Mahendra's land-reform policy 1960s also encouraged more hill people to move to Terai. By then, people of Indian origin, mainly from nearby Bihar, UP (Utter Pradesh) and other parts of India, had migrated to Nepal in big numbers and occupied the vast empty and fertile lands of Terai. The open-border policy and its proximity to India helped develop the region as the main gateway to India.

I travelled from the east to the west through the Terai plains in 2018 on a research trip for my previous book and had the opportunity to see the life those people in Terai had, at least from the surface. The first noticeable difference was the unlikeliness and dissimilarity between the people here and those on the hills. They were more like the Indians than the Nepalis, and one could easily mistake them for Indians. I genuinely felt like I was in a foreign country, which was a strange feeling for me, and I wasn't alone in feeling that way. If there was a reason for calling them 'Madhesi' and the hill people 'Pahadi', this must be the main one.

In the 1970s and 1980s, as a Pahadi, I had seen them, the Madhesis, working on all the odd jobs in cities like Kathmandu and Pokhara, and never thought they happened to be Nepali of Indian origin from the Terai. They came with their old cycle, collected bottles and plastic cans, and sold peanuts, ice cream, and sweat. Others came pushing wooden carts selling everything—fruits, vegetables, clothes, plastic jerricans, toys, and cheap household products on roadsides, junctions and outside cinema halls. They also worked on construction sites especially fixing the kitchen and bathroom in a new house. Whether it was a barber, a dressmaker, or a sweetmaker, that required a little bit of skill, it was all done by the Madhesis, and all the Pahadis did was buy from them. Today, every business, big or small in Nepal, is run by the Madhesis or the people of Indian origin, and the Pahadis are still buying everything from them as they have from the start. Still, the Pahadis always had an aura of superiority over the Madhesis. They used to call them by derogatory names like 'Dhoti' (loin cloth), but 'Bhaiya' (brother) was/is an acceptable and commonly used term.

The fundamental problem here is not about being a Madhesi or a Pahadi; instead, it's the epic failure of integration of the two communities, and both are equally responsible for not trying. Both sides look at each other with suspicion: one as India's proxy and the other as a bully, creating a perennial mistrust between the two communities. Other than business interactions, they hardly talk, work, live together, or allow intermarriage between the two communities, and yet the Madhesi leaders' actions have made the Pahadis even more suspicious. They regularly visit the corridors of power in Delhi, Patna, and Lucknow and openly advocate India's interests in Nepal as their own. They initiated several movements in the 1970s and 1980s in the name of an identity crisis, and openly asked for India's intervention whenever the actions didn't bring a satisfying result.

The Madhesi community might have been experiencing genuine grievances. Still, they ruined their chances by openly calling for and facilitating the Indian blockade in 2015 against the new constitution, claiming it claiming treated them unfairly and lost all the sympathy the Pahadis and the country had for them.

India's tried and tested policy of using the Madhesi people against Nepal is another thorn in the Nepal-India relationship. India has never hesitated to use this readymade tool whenever it is unhappy with Nepal. The Madhesi community has also acted chiefly like they were from the other side of the border and showed where their loyalty lies. The Terai, comprising 51 per cent of the population, represents only 17 per cent of the country's land mass. In contrast, the hills, with 49 per cent of the people, hold 83 per cent of areas of the country—they argued. As a result, they should have been awarded more seats in the parliament, and this was the leading cause of their dissatisfaction. They forget that the trees made up the forest and missed the point that the hills were mostly made of cliffs, gorges, slopes and inhospitable terrains. Instead of asking for division and sharing, they should discuss integration and cooperation and start working together for the country's well-being as a team.

The Nepali people have never forgotten the two blockades that India imposed on Nepal. To express its displeasure over King Birendra's purchase of military arms and ammunition from China, India imposed a year-long blockade in 1989. Similarly, India imposed another six-month-long blockade in 2015 upon the request of the Madhesi leaders to express their unhappiness towards Nepal's new constitution. The blockades had a severe impact on the Nepali people's daily lives, and they have not forgotten about it. The perennial harassments by the Indian security forces against the Nepali villagers at border areas is nothing new. They are notorious for regularly moving the border pillars to encroach on Nepali lands. When we were at Puranbas border town, Kanchanpur, in 2018, we saw the white cement border pillars right next to the town area, which according to the villagers, used to be on the other side of the forest just a few months ago. Encroaching on Nepali land by moving the pillar is standard practice on the border, and they do it mainly at night, we were told. The Indian security forces have also beaten up Nepali villagers who have complained, and local newspapers carry such news regularly.

The Indian security forces bullying tactics at the border have irked the Nepali people, and the indifference and inaction from the Nepali government further angered them. An incident that showed how the Indian security force acted with impunity and had sheer disregard for the Nepali life was when a Nepali migrant worker crossing a single-rope bridge over the Mahakali River in west Nepal lost his life after an Indian security guard mercilessly cut off the rope. Another innocent young man lost his life when the Indian side used explosives at the border area without warning, and the debris hit the unfortunate boy. The whole nation cried out foul and demonstrated against the Indian's reckless act. But of course, nothing happened—nobody aplogised nor was anyone compensated. Yet, such incidents managed to send out a message-'India always gets away with anything'—people better start believing this.

A similar story of India's infringement upon the Nepali border is making news in the Nepali media as I write these words. India has been building an embarkment on Kali River at Dharchula, Khalanga Western Nepal, for the last two years that will eventually change the course of the river towards Nepal. Dissatisfied by India's unilateral action, locals gathered on the Nepali side of the river and started pelting stones to show their anger. The other side retaliated with the same force injuring at least four on the Nepali side. People from various parts of Nepal demanded action from the government, but nothing will come out of it as usual. Any complaints from the

Nepali side will end up to a deaf ear, and Delhi will carry on doing whatever it has planned, and the Nepali elites will not even utter a word against it.

Another reason that irritates the Nepali is India's policy of micromanaging, putting its nose in almost everywhere, and telling Nepalis how to live their lives. Indian ambassadors are the busiest in Kathmandu, for they used to attend Nepal's cabinet meetings regularly. The embassy staffs are seen active almost everywhere in Nepal. Whether it is a water project, cultural program, political event, governmental office, road and bridge project, land and forest development, a student program, religious procession, or social and economic gathering, they must be there. It's a common practice in Kathmandu for Nepali leaders to consult the Indian ambassador before making any essential appointments, such as the police and army chief of Nepal. It's not me making these up—a former Indian ambassador to Nepal wrote them in his last book.

The Indians are also allergic to everything about the Chinese, especially the Indian media. One only needs to say the word 'China' and they all come out straight at you, attacking from all directions like a hoard of angry hornets. They also come up with all sorts of conspiracy theories fit to outsmart the best conspirators in the world. For instance, when the Chinese helped build the Ring Road in Kathmandu, the Indian media said the Chinese wanted to land a fighter plane there. China made the Kathmandu-Kodari Highway linking Kathmandu to Lhasa, to move tanks from China to Nepal and India. In his recent visit to Nepal, Indian Prime Minister Modi didn't fly into the airport at Lumbini simply because the Chinese built it, but they were okay with having a Chinese company make and fix the head of Sardar Vallavbhai Patel's statue at Sardar Sarovar Dam in Gujarat, India.

Whenever Chinese companies win a tender in Nepal, the whole Indian media goes into a frenzy and asks many questions as if Nepal were one of their union territories. They think Nepal has a moral responsibility to ask for India's permission before committing anything to anyone, and when they don't get the answer, they punish Nepal with a blockade. And this is where the Indians have it all wrong, for this is not the best way to win over a friend. Although small, weak, and poor, Nepal is still a sovereign country, and one must always remember that fact.

Nepali people, in general, have also not forgotten about the unfair treatment of the Gorkhas in Northeast India during the 1980s and 1990s, where several states had failed to protect them from the unlawful persecution, displacement, and confiscation of their properties. Failing to heed the Gorkha's aspiration of a separate state within India's constitution is another sign of India's total disregard, indifference and respect for the Nepali people. India's inhumane and irresponsible behaviours towards the Bhutanese refugees of Nepali origin further dented its reputation as a caring neighbour, and the possibility of Sikkimization of Nepal is another factor that has robbed many periods of sleep out of many Nepalis' life. Yet, India has done almost nothing to alleviate such fears to show the Nepali people that they are good friends of Nepal. Until India stops taking Nepal for granted and tries to show its good intention, the fear, suspicion and dislike of Nepali people towards India will remain.

Nepal is a small country between two giants—India and China. Due to its geographical position and also the similarity in language, culture, religion and way of life, Nepal is closer to India. But Nepal should have a balanced relationship between India and China for the country's sake—it should never neglect its ties with China. Why is that crucial? Here is the reason. When India finally got its independence from the British, leaders in the corridor of power in Delhi floated the idea of including Nepal within its union territories. Even Nehru admitted that as he addressed the parliament,

Savarkar openly advocated for it. Believe it or not, it was the China factor that forced them to abandon the idea and leave Nepal alone for good. Perturbed by the newly formed Communist government in China, the US and the Western power were worried and did everything to stop communism from spreading to other parts of the world. The last thing they wanted was communist China bordering democratic India, and Nepal's strategic position fitted perfectly as a buffer zone between China and India. The Americans vetoed the idea, and the Indian leaders had to listen to big brother. It was the main reason why India established seventeen military checkposts along the Chinese border at the Himalayas.

Nepal was able to to continue as a sovereign country for that reason, and that logic is as crucial today as it was then. The Americans might have a different reason today to have Nepal on its side, for they are not afraid of communism as they were in the early 1950s. Today both China and America are vying for world dominance, and America wants to use Nepal to contain its main rival—China.

The rivalry between China and India has become so crucial today that China won't stay quiet if India tries anything to change the status quo regarding Nepal. Despite its geographical, political, economic, and social dominance over Nepal, India cannot do much as far as Nepal's sovereignty is concerned, and Nepal should never forget this. It was China that saved Nepal before, and it will also be China that will save Nepal in the future. A life lesson every Nepali should never forget.

The Roles and Responsibilities of the Nepali Leadership

'If he is alone, he becomes a poet, but once he is joined by one of his friends, they turn to politicians.' This is a famous saying in Nepal for a reason—talking about politics is a national hobby of Nepal, and they celebrate the election as if it was a festival. The way Indians are crazy about cricket and Bollywood, Nepalis are obsessed with politics, and people who lack an interest in politics will have difficulty finding new friends. At home, offices, or other gatherings, politics are the main topic they all discuss, and they also make friends according to the taste of their political preferences. Writers, lawyers, business people, teachers, shopkeepers, medical professionals, mechanics, engineers, farmers, students, homemakers, security guards and so on, no matter their profession, they can quickly get into a serious political discussion and express their views. A neighbourhood tea stall is a much loved place for having such political discourses and enjoying by all participants and the audiences simultaneously.

Election season in Nepal is fervently awaited by all and celebrated as one of its big festivals. In anticipation of the final Election Day, people start debating it in great detail weeks before and keep on counting the day with more heated discussions. People gather at homes, offices, teashops, and cafes and talk passionately about politics. They also pick sides and fight and argue relentlessly for their political belief. The argument continues at the office, home, and public places. The loudest, most intense and bitter fighting usually takes place on social media, and people have been seen fighting with their best friends and loved ones because of their political views. The nation gets involved in the festive mood during the election and keeps talking about it long after it has been done and dusted. In other words, everyone in Nepal is an expert in politics, yet they always have little to show. Unfortunately, Nepal mostly has a plethora of selfish, greedy, corrupted, shameless, unreliable, and spineless leaders who always put their interests before the country. Its neverending search for a charismatic, strong, and respectable leader is still on.

Apart from King Prithvi Narayan (the founder of Nepal) and King Mahendra (who set the stone for developing a new Nepal), most Nepali leadership have failed the country. King Mahendra was the only leader in Nepal's history who defied the American and the Indians, initiated a deal with China with a whopping no-string attached to a grant of $126 million, and managed to balance two superpowers for the sake of Nepal's interest. After Kind Tribhuwan signed the momentous General Agreement for Technical Cooperation between Nepal and the US in 1951 in Delhi, the US launched an aggressive foreign aid and development agenda in Nepal.

The Nepali Congress Party has been on its payroll since then. The US support to Nepal ended in 1972 after its relationship with China improved, which prompted its policy change towards China. The Sino-US relationship remained calm and normal throughout the eighties, nineties and 2000s, and so were the US involvements in Nepal. With the recent changes in the US policy towards they suddenly realised the importance of Nepal's geographically strategic position and started ramping up their activities in Nepal.

Among them, the controversial implementation of the $500 million MCC (Millennium Challenge Corporation) was Nepal's most hated and debated US project.

The East-West Highway that extends across Nepal is still the main highway that connects all Nepalis today. It was actually built by King Mahendra and affectionately called the 'Mahendra Highway'. King Mahendra also introduced a new policy in the sixties when people from the hills were encouraged to migrate to the border areas of the southern plains by allocating free lands under the resettlement programmes. People migrating from the hills could occupy as much land as they could till and start a new residence as they liked. Had it not been for his forward-thinking, Nepal's southern borders might have been in a different shape and location today. I had the privilege of visiting those resettled villages and travelling through the highway from the eastern to the western parts of Nepal in 2018. Decades later, people still take advantage of the fruits of his far-sightedness and vision, and Nepalis should remain eternally grateful to him. Despite being autocratic, he was a good and visionary leader.

Being one of the most beautiful countries in the world, replete with an abundance of natural resources, Nepal still lingers at the bottom as one of the poor, weak, and undeveloped countries of the world. With zero industry, and no FDI (foreign direct investment), the economy hangs on remittance. With no job and no roadmap for future development, Nepal's future is as bleak and uncertain as it was decades before, and the country's youths have no choice but to go to a foreign country for a better opportunity. Believe it or not, Nepali youths are the only viable export the government has today, and one cannot take it as a proud moment of the country no matter from which aspect you look into it. The obvious question one should ask is who is responsible for all this. Of course, the answer is more complex than it might seem, but most of the blames must go to the Nepali leadership, including the present day's ones.

Foreign powers have played crucial roles in the making and breaking Nepal; there is no doubt about that. But blaming the foreigners alone won't wash away the Nepali leaders' sins. Besides, the leaders were the ones who allowed/allowing foreign interventions primarily for personal gains. The Ranas were the worst culprit, and their 105 years long regime was the darkest period in Nepal. The way they treated the people and plundered the country's assets was beyond words. No matter how you condemn them, it will never be enough, and the crimes they committed against the country and the people of Nepal should never be forgotten or forgiven by the Nepali people.

As the saying goes, history is there for the new generations to see and learn from, so it won't repeat itself, especially the wrong ones. People may have a short memory span and learning from the past is not our strong point. Nepal is no exception; it has learned almost nothing from its past mistakes. Having an evil, selfish and corrupted leader was predestined in the Nepali people's fate. But blaming the leaders alone won't solve Nepal's problems. Nepali people must know what they want in a leader and select the right one for the country's sake.

If we ask this question to the Nepali general public, we will probably get a wide variety of answers. But the most popular solutions would be something like these—he has to be strong, charismatic and visionary. An honest, proud and above materialistic values; wise, disciplinarian, and powerful enough to say no to foreign powers; intelligent, decisive, and down to earth with experience and skills to deal on the international stage; a good, fair and uncorrupted one; an educated, thoughtful and respectful man; and the list goes on. But it's impossible to find such an ideal and capable leader who can solve all Nepal's problems as if he has a magic wand in his hand and waving it a few more times would make everything go away. That's not happening as we all live in the real world, and we must think as rationally as otherworldly people do here.

In search of an ideal leader, Nepali people cannot be too fussy, greedy, or over-ambitious as they have already wasted much more time than they deserve. What Nepal needs is a simple, honest, and honourable leader with knowledge on both national and international levels, good oratory skills, understanding economy and is good at numbers, experience in management and a knack for problem-solving, good decision making and balls to tell as it is, and incorruptible. Most importantly, he must talk less and work more, has the trust and respect of the general public, and loves the country more than anything else. Since this will be impossible to find all these virtues in a single leader, Nepal will need a group of leaders blessed with similar views and characters and be able to work cohesively together as a unified team. They must have the same faith, belief and goal and put the nation's interest before anything else.

The collective team of leadership must represent each community of the country and safeguard their interests at the national level so that every community will be included. Nepal still suffers from the feudal caste system, and discrimination between the different communities is still rife. In the name of religious freedom and century-long culture, one community mustn't allow infringing on the liberty and sentiment of other communities, and every different neighbourhood within the country should be tolerated if not respected. Having a representative of their own on a national level guarantees each community of their rights, values and share of fruits. In the long run, it avoids possible dissent and friction among the communities, bringing much-needed stability and harmony to the nation.

The country's leadership must avoid idolising a particular leader within the community, for too much respect, trust or responsibility to a person can be too risky for the country. The practice could also make a man God, and he will start behaving like one. He will also attract yes-men-like flies and change to a despot. A man holding too much power with impunity can be too dangerous to any country. Power must be centralised to a certain number of institutions with a collective leadership. They must create strong institutions, not individuals, so that personnel at the top can be replaced without affecting the smooth running of important country institutions.

Although institutions like public transport and healthcare could be run as private enterprises, they have to be affordable. The education system must be recalibrated with theoretical, practical, ethical, and liberal studies. Engineering, mechanical, technical and vocational institutes have to be prioritised. Opportunities for business and entrepreneurship in any industry must be encouraged. The state must be ready to help them by creating a business-friendly environment and policy within the nation. The civil servants must cut out all the bureaucracy and red tape, becoming faithful public servants as they were supposed to be. Government officials must be paid well and trained to do well in their jobs. They are here to serve the public, not the other way around, and they must get this basic message first before they start working. Failing to heed the message should result in disqualification.

The country's disciplinarian services, such as the army, police, custom, and fire department, must be well-trained, well-equipped, and well-funded. They must also be independent, disciplined, organised, and kept out of politics. Most importantly, they must be free of political interference and allowed to perform their duties, such as safeguarding national security and defence, maintaining public laws and orders, saving public lives and eradicating illegal activities and other vices within the communities.

The leadership should create a situation where people from every race and community feel connected; their political, social and cultural interests are respected, and they never felt neglected or left out. The sense of involvement and participation is a big motivator, and people can achieve miracles in such situations. Similarly, all races, creeds, and religions of people must be accepted, and their traditions, cultures, and values are equally observed from the eyes of the authority. No one should be discriminated against based on their gender, faith, and skin colour. Everybody from the community should have a say in the decision-making involving their community. In short, they must be included in contributing and rewarding processes and ultimately responsible for their actions.

The country should implement a new system where every person, position, and project is selected not on personal connection and interest but on merit. A vetting process should be applied when choosing the right person for a job of higher importance. Members from all the communities should be allowed to participate, provided the candidates are qualified. Talks alone won't change anything, people must start actual work, and accountability is a serious problem that needs to be solved in the country. Everybody must start pitching in their share of contribution to the country.

The country should also create an atmosphere where people in such fields as art, literature, music, and sport are encouraged by the community and can chase them as careers. They should be pursued as a passion and profession, for it's the country's soul and can motivate people to achieve great things. Countries without artists, musicians, and writers are like a body without a soul; one cannot expect much from such countries in the real world.

They also help keep the country sane in difficult times and entertain and motivate it in good times. They are also probably the ones who might help introduce the country to the international stage and make the nation proud. In other words, they teach us how to live and love our country. People also need a regular dose of their artistic creations to deal with the travails of their daily life.

They should appropriately regulate the financial and tax system. All taxes are to be properly levied and collected, and tax evaders severely punished. The country's imports and export must be balanced, FDIs encouraged, and a policy of tax concession should be provided to first-time businesses. Similarly, people who have professional skills from the Nepali diaspora should be welcomed back. The country must be ready to listen to their advice and adopt them if they help improve the situation. In appreciation of their contribution, if necessary, the authority shouldn't hesitate to offer them key positions to retain those talents and take full advantage of their expertise for the country's sake. These are the people who have seen the world, worked with and learned from some of the best on the job, and can play a significant role in teaching and mentoring the young in their respective fields. Besides, they would be coming back for much more critical factors than money and willing to give it their best.

Nepal needs more solid governmental institutions. Public institutions such as transport, healthcare, and education are the backbone of a country and should be operated and regulated correctly by relevant governmental departments. On the contrary, everything in Nepal, including those crucial institutions, is run by cartels. Such essential aspects as good service and public safety are the last thing they have in mind. In short, everything has become business with a singular mission to make money. Private schools, private hospitals, and private transportation sprouted everywhere like mushrooms. Quality got replaced by vanity, the achievement was overshadowed by status, and decency was overtaken by excess. As a result, everything becomes too expensive and out of reach for ordinary people, making people angry and frustrated.

After all, they were supposed to be essential services that the government should have provided to its people for an affordable cost. Politicians' involvement is the main reason behind these illicit practices, and the public knows those cartels would have never flourished without the blessings of the country's top leaders. Such practices by the country's leaders are morally wrong and a crime against the country. The country's leaders must stop making money at the expense of the country and its people and start putting people's interests before their own.

It's a common belief in Nepal that most of the country's leaders have connections with India's powerful political and religious parties. Some of the country's former prime ministers' old and new alike, are even accused of being members of India's intelligence agencies. For instance, Dr Tulsi Giri, the first Panchayati Prime Minister, was a member of the Rashtriya Swayamsevak Sangh (RSS), and other leaders from different political parties were labelled as foreign assets. Even some Nepalis believe India was in cahoots with the Maoists, for it wouldn't have been possible to wage such a long and deadly insurgency against a nation with a substantial army force without India's support.

Unsurprisingly, Nepali leaders hardly attempt to quell such rumours and continue pretending they are cleanest of them all in Nepali politics. If they are to have the respect and trust of the public, Nepali leaders should pay more attention to their reputation and try to work hard to keep that clean image for a long time. One can never become a good leader with a foreign stooge tag hanging over their name.

Most importantly, the leadership must create enough jobs here in the country, so the country's youths don't have to go outside. A country whose most precious assets, its youth, don't value and respect the county cannot expect a promising future, and one must stop such an unfortunate situation at the earliest. This can be achieved if everyone from the country comes together by putting their differences and interests aside and working together for the country's sake. The country must also re-educate its new generations and instil a new sense of patriotism and belonging, so they start loving their country very early. If the country is strong, united, and self-reliant, people will start feeling proud of their country and start thinking about the country more passionately. Besides a good job, a lovely house, and comfortable living, dignity is the most precious factor in life, and people always prefer to live a dignified life. Only a rich, solid, and successful country can provide that privilege on the international stage, and the new leadership must be able to unite the whole country and motivate them to work towards that one important goal.

The Gorkhas' Future

The Gorkhas are by nature simple, straightforward, and less educated. They don't like serious matters and prefer joking, jesting, and partying around. Brought up in a relatively lenient but closely-knitted family, they are rather communal and mainly perceived as honest people. Before they found themselves very good at soldiering, they earned their living through farming and animal husbandry. Once the British saw their pedigree as one of the best soldiers in the world, they had been making this trade for the last two centuries and hardly tried anything else. It's improbable for the Gorkhas to be involved in other occupations and professions other than soldiering, which has created a bigger problem for them. When the opportunity of soldiering became scarcer, they couldn't find anything else to do, for they had already become a one-trick pony; hence, the skill that made them famous also became a liability.

After the sun had finally set on the British Empire, the Gorkhas that were recruited in the British army in recent years were just a few hundred, but over twenty thousand youths compete for the few hundred posts. A little over 2,000 youths join the Indian Gorkha yearly. Millions of Nepali youths work as cheap labourers around the globe without a formal contract, protection, or insurance. Another hundred thousand cross the Nepal-India border yearly and work in lowly paid, unsafe, and exploited conditions. Some of the unfortunate ones take the illegal route, are preyed upon by human traffickers, and end up losing their lives.

Today, pockets of the Nepali/Gorkhali community are scattered around the globe. USA, Canada, the UK, Europe, Australia, New Zealand, Europe, Hong Kong, Singapore, Malaysia, Thailand, Myanmar, S. Korea, Japan, the Middle East, you name it, and they are almost everywhere. The first generations might return to Nepal from time to time as they still hold some properties in Nepal, but the new generations raised and educated in those foreign countries hardly have any connections or attachment to their motherland and will find no reasons to return. Over time, they will have a real problem calling themselves Nepali, Gorkhali, British, American, Canadian, or their country's name. The dilemma they could face regarding the lost identity is all but confirmed. Once they have nothing to return home to, they will have no reasons to send the money to Nepal. Without the remittance money, the country's economy will stagnate, which spells a bigger problem for Nepal and can severely impact its future.

Unfortunately, the Gorkhas are probably the only people with cemeteries in countries such as the UK, Belgium, Germany, France, Italy, the Middle East, Africa, India, Myanmar, Malaysia, Singapore, and Hong Kong, and the prospect of changing that situation is almost nonexistent. Over 100,000 Gorkhas serve in the Indian army, and they have always been the first ones to fight on the battlefields if war breaks out, and many have lost their lives over border struggles with Pakistan and China. They have shed blood in many theatres of war within India, including Sri Lanka.

After sacrificing their best years to a foreign country, they return home and pick up the life they had left behind when they went to join a foreign army. The meagre pension they get in return is hardly enough to get by with the new life, forcing them to seek out for an alternative way to compensate the shortage again. Before long, they will work in a foreign land as security personnel again. After a few trips back home and forth, he will be either too old or a sick man with not much time left in this world. Yet, not much has improved back in his village. Only one thing is guaranteed. Just like him and many more before him, his son (if he one) will take his place and take the same route as he has done. The tradition must continue, after all. Blame it on anyone, including themselves, but the practice must continue.

Over ten million Gorkhas currently live in various parts of India, and they have been subjected to many types of discrimination, racism, and persecution over time. Despite legally residing in India, they have to prove their identity repeatedly and have continuously experienced harassment, mockery and unfair treatment from most Indians. Whenever ethnic violence flares up between rival communities, the Gorkhas get punished and face physical violence, looting, and displacement from their homes. Political parties have always taken them for granted. For them, the Gorkhas are nothing more than a vote bank that's useful only when there are elections. Other times, they can be used and tossed up for pleasure. The relevant authorities (both central and state governments) have also applied indifferent, apathetic, and ambivalent policies towards the Gorkhas and failed to protect them as the state should have done for its subjects, abandoning them to the mercy of the perpetrators most often.

The Gorkhas usually join the British and Indian army at eighteen, and they are about thirty-three to forty years old after they retire from the army services. That's a good age for the start of a second career, and they usually seek out one. However, since they don't know anything other than carrying a rifle, they have only two choices—to work in the field or go outside to find a job in the security services.

Since working on the farm does not yield much, they mostly choose the latter option and go outside to work in war-torn countries like Iraq, Syria, Afghanistan, Hong Kong, Brunei, Malaysia, and other Gulf nations. In the process of finding a new job, they often end up spending their lifesaving, forced to then work for another ten to twenty years to recover that money. By the time they finish working, they are already too old with all the diseases men can have, and their remaining years are spent visiting the doctor's door.

The *Lahure* tradition (joining the British and the Indian armies) that started two hundred years ago is still just as strong today as it was then. Pardon me, but this is not something that Nepal should be proud. Instead, Nepal should feel sorry for not being able to find an alternative way for this *Lahure* tradition. Similarly, Gorkhas in the Northeast region of India still depend on cow-herding today as they did two centuries ago. Many generations might have come and gone in two hundred years, and if one cannot improve their way of life for such an extended period, one must realise where the problem lies.

The British sent *Gallawalas* (Gorkha recruitment agents) to Nepal to get their men, followed by the Indians, and the two-century-old tradition is still alive today. What's more, *Gallawalas* from other countries such as the US, Canada, Australia, Europe, and Gulf nations have also started working in Nepal and turned the country into a talent pool from where they can fill up their needs of the workforce in both skilled and unskilled markets. The practice has become so prevalent that only a few youths with a sound education, ability, and ambition would like to remain in Nepal, making securing an overseas job the main dream of youths in Nepal. Representatives from those countries openly advocate their trade through projects sponsoring, NGOs, and donations, and offer their needs as opportunities, making it look like they were doing a favour to Nepal. Nepal's severe brain drain issue can cause disastrous consequences shortly, but nobody seems to care about it.

The old *Lahures* are replaced by the new *Lahures* now. Nepal's youths go to any country that welcomes them and willingly accept any job offer. Many go through manpower agencies; others go through connections with foreign institutions, work and student visas, and family relations. Those desperate ones try illegally, seek asylum, and apply for lottery visas to get out of the country. The country has no jobs, no value for its youths, and no rules of law, opportunity, and justice for the poor. A country that sells its youths and survives on remittance money has no right to dream big. The leaders are selfish, greedy, shameless, and spineless, and so busy enriching themselves that the country is the last thing they have in mind. Nobody gets into politics to build the country; instead, they enter politics to plunder and get rich quickly. Even worse, leaders never have to lift a finger in the name of nation-building. All they need to do is talk, for talking alone is enough here as they never have to show proof of work. Nobody ever asks how we arrived in such a dire situation, and with such a mentality, everything will stay the same in the next 1000 years.

Nepal has seen cultural awareness in recent years but not intellectual and political understanding, thanks to Western donors. Nepal's indigenous people were used in the name of cultural value, and a new word such as Shetamagurali (Sherpa, Tamang, Magar, Gurung, Rai and Limbu) appeared. But it failed to improve their livelihood. This has done more harm than good to the community, bringing more division and suspicion. The passage of Christianity in the Nepali community was just an extension of the tried and tested old divide-and-rule policy by the Western powers, and they have succeeded in many ways. With some strong dollars, not only did Christianity get a foothold in Nepal but also flourished at the expense of the peaceful Hindu/Buddhist coexistence. When will people in Nepal understand the mantra of no free lunch in this world? Everybody wants something in return for their investment, and one has to pay the due sooner or later.

The community is also suffering from an inferior-complex

mentality that gives a false impression that they are, in fact, well-off. Community members will only do such jobs as watchmen, bodyguards, housekeeping, street cleaners, servants, and other manual workers. They are ashamed of taking such jobs as they think it's below them and will lose face in society if they get involved in such lowly jobs. Nobody should have any problem with that attitude. After all, life is all about aiming high. But the irony is somewhat cynical. Those odd jobs they are so ashamed of doing back in Nepal are the same jobs these people do abroad, and you don't see them complaining about that. They lack the necessary skill, experience]and qualifications to land a well-paid job in the offices and other fields. That raises an obvious question: If you can take those jobs abroad, why can't they be done back home?

Another reason why Gorkhas primarily end up working in such lowly jobs abroad is the lack of relevant training back home before going abroad. The irresponsible government washes its hands of all the responsibilities and does almost nothing for the sake of its people, allowing greedy and unscrupulous agencies to make all the arrangements. When one country imports workers (skilled/unskilled) from another country, there should be a treaty highlighting all terms and regulations regarding the monthly salary, working conditions, workers' rights, safety measurements, and severance pay in case of unfortunate incidents where one gets injured or killed, just to ensure all parties abide by the international laws. Workers also should be trained in the necessary skills and familiarise with the language, tradition, culture, and rules of law of their destination country before their departure. But of course, no such treaty or precautions are taken in Nepal, and unregulated agencies use anything, including illegal ways, to make money. As a result, many Gorkhas end up in the wrong places and suffer unimaginable tragedies where they get used, misused. and exploited. Some unlucky ones have ended up paying with their lives.

Just imagine the scenario—a young man who hasn't even been out of his village suddenly finds himself in a foreign country with different people, languages, cultures, and ways of life. Not many people can handle such an amount of shock, making them extremely weak and vulnerable. Until the government comes up with a formal agreement with the foreign countries and provides necessary training before their departure, the suffering and exploitation of the Gorkhas abroad won't end.

The world never stops revolving, and neither do human beings. Powerful countries don't have to send troops with guns anymore to colonise other weaker nations. Colonisation through the mind and ideology is more effective and long-lasting and provides multiple options. Movie, literature, music, culture, religion, education, fashion, sport, and food are the primary mediums through which powerful countries expand their dominance to other parts of the world. Still, language is the most powerful tool that helps spread its influence over other people, communities, and countries. English can be a typical example of how it influences people's lives. The effects on poorer and weaker countries that don't have their own strong culture, history, tradition, and a sense of belonging are the most vulnerable ones as they are more prone to outside influences than those rich and established countries. On top of those soft approaches, powerful countries also use physical methods in the name of aid, donations, loans, and other initiatives. It's the main reason youngsters from poor nations have idols from western countries, and why they watch Hollywood, listen to pop music, read western books, eat McDonald's, and drink Coca-Cola, and believe in everything the western narratives tell them.

If you are in Kathmandu, you might quickly notice the omnipresence of foreigners and their involvement in everything in Nepal. The embassy staff, INGOs, and other foreign institutions are almost everywhere. Diplomats in foreign countries behave somewhat cautiously and discreetly, for they wouldn't want be seen interfering in the host nation's internal affairs. Appearing in the local media with an opinion is a big no unless one wants to stir up things intentionally and face the consequences. On the contrary, foreigners here in Nepal talk, work, and write openly. Mainstream newspapers and social media are full of them attending the opening ceremony, discussing with intellectuals and community leaders, and meeting the country's top leaders. So much so that there is hardly a single project in Kathmandu without foreign involvement and hardly any individuals with no connection with foreign institutions. It felt like nothing ever happened in Kathmandu without those foreigners, making one wonder who the boss was here. Let me be frank here and ask you this simple question—if you cannot run your own house, what's the use of having one?

The foreigners are here to implement their policy and protect their interests by colonising your mind through ideology and offering other incentives such as donations, aid, and other opportunities. They have various tools at their disposal, and dangling carrots in front of the poor is the most effective way. They want you to be weak, poor, and dependent so they can manipulate you to their liking. They want you to adopt their ideology, culture, beliefs, religion, and way of life. The world is cruel, there is no such thing as a free lunch, and one has to pay for it one way or another. At the end of the day, it's all about power, position, and money, and the foreigners can only lord Nepalis around as long as they remain poor and weak; it's all about dominance. Unless the entire Nepali population has no self-respect, dignity, and honour, this shameless, disgraceful, and subservient act of the nation must stop.

Most importantly, the Gorkha community must put an end to the baneful tradition of drinking, partying, and indulging in the pursuit of entertainment all their life. The community must start to unite and work together for its well-being, instead of being individualistic. The new changes must come from home, and sons and daughters must be treated equally. Parents must start sending their children to the library, not the *libary* (singing and dancing), give priority to education, not entertainment, and must teach them the basics of ethics, discipline, and the elements of being a decent and responsible person. The new generations must also learn the skill of working together in a group and understand the power of unity as a community and a country. Children also must learn not to be selfish, self-centred, and shortsightedness. They must be taught about the importance of education, self-reliance, and their duty and responsibility towards their community and, eventually, their country. New generations must know that the secret to long-term happiness and prosperity in life is being able to feel and share the achievements with your people and be proud of what you are, which is impossible unless you love and respect them. Only then will an individual, a community, and a country prosper.

Nepal needs a revolution of not guns but the mentality to get out of this lull. And it must start with the new generation, from their home, school, temple, and the community all at once. They must be taught to love their people, community and country; must know how to differentiate between nationalism and patriotism; must learn to be caring, disciplined, and responsible; must have both theoretical and practical education; must learn to hate discrimination, racism, and unfair treatment; must get rid of bribery, cronyism, and favouritism; must learn to differentiate between respect and popularity, entitlement and hard work, and self-respect and ego; must understand rights, equality, and duty of individuals in the county; must learn to believe in actions, not words; must stop idolising individual by believing in the vital institution; and start loving and believing in oneself before anything else. Most importantly, you must stop being selfish, know the power of unity, and never become a sell-out; see the value of your country and your identity; put your people and country above anything else; and learn the meaning of living a simple, dignified, and honourable life.

In just fifteen years, the revolution could be finished for the new generations to eventually take over the reins of the country. It doesn't mean the country will become wealthy, self-reliant, and successful by then. What it means is changes will start appearing from then on, and the country will start climbing up the success ladder for good. As we have already discussed in the previous chapter, Nepal is a blessed country with abundant natural resources; all it needs to do is do one thing and do it properly. Nepal has thousands of big and small rivers with vast estuaries with the potential to produce over 80,000 megawatts (MW) of hydropower. Nepal currently produces a meagre 1500 MW and imports electricity from India. Nepal can develop its full hydropower potential into electricity and make everything they do in Nepal powered by electricity. Using electric cars, electronic household items, offices, roads, fields, schools, businesses, and switch to everything that could make them electricity-friendly. Extra electricity could be sold to neighbouring countries and the money could be used to balance out the country's import-export market. The country is already beautiful and could be even more eco-friendly and healthy. People will live longer and happier, and thus be more productive, and Nepal will never have to beg for foreign donations again. You, the sons of the Gorkhas, are world-known for your bravery and you could be known as an honourable people too; you could live a dignified life in a sovereign country for good.

The time for singing about Gorkha's bravery is gone. It's time for the Gorkha community to know their history, talk about their contributions, and ask for their rights. One must never forget that Nepal's history is incomplete without the Gorkha's history, and the country must learn to appreciate their contributions. The Gorkha's enlistment into the British Indian army was one of the reasons why the British did not come to Kathmandu during the Anglo-Gorkha War of 1814-16. The official sanctioning of the Gorkha's enlistment into the British Indian army in 1885 by Bir Shamsher prevented the British from heading to Kathmandu again with troops. Chandra Shamsher sent over 200,000 Gorkhas to fight for the British during the First World War to give Nepal respect and prestige as a sovereign country. Another 250,000 Gorkha fought for the British again in the Second World War during Juddha Shamsher's reign, in order to legalise Nepal's membership in the international community. The Gorkhas furnished freedom fighters and fought against the Nepal Army to end the 105-year-long Rana autocracy, bringing democracy to Nepal for the very first time. Those were Gorkha's contributions that historians still need to register and the country needs to recognise. They cannot ignore it anymore, and the Gorkhas must get the respect and recognition they deserve without delays.

The country is much bigger than internal feuds, personal interests, and communal division. If people keep fighting over trivial issues, the outer forces, more organised and robust, will get the upper hand, and what's the use of small wins when you end up losing your own country? Let's pause and think about it—it's called the big picture. Please try to understand it.

Nepal desperately needs one thing that can unite the whole nation. Something huge and profoundly powerful that can connect, inspire, and pull the entire country in a single direction. For instance, a football team can participate internationally and can win games and shine all at the same time. Perhaps we need a Nepal football team playing in the World Cup and carrying the hope and dream of the entirety of Nepal as never before. Such a miracle alone could make every Nepali proud and happy for good and could save the country. Let's hope and pray for the country.

★★★

The Gorkha Grief

The Gorkha grief might not be limited to the Gorkhas who had been serving foreign powers other than their own country for over two centuries. Still, it all started from their sufferings and struggles and extended to other Gorkhalis who followed the same route, albeit for a different purpose. Whereas many Gorkhas left their homeland for soldiering, others came out of their country in search of a better life. They were involved in several jobs: farmers, animal rearers, railway and roadway workers, security guards, gardeners, oil and mine workers, house servants, porters, cattle grazers, and manual labourers. Regardless of their work or profession, they all share the same grief.

Systematic exploitation, discrimination, and unfair treatment, the pain of being far away from home, insecurity and fear, humiliation and abuse, bodily harm and mental torture, stigmatisation and insult, racism and inequality, dishonour and indignity, loss of identity, and having to live in a constant pressure as a second-class citizen were some of the few grievances they faced abroad. Betrayed by destiny, abandoned by their people, and exploited and used by others, the Gorkha experiences are a tragedy that others have flagrantly ignored. The Gorkhas have failed to admit their fate, let alone comprehend it. This book will not only try its best to highlight the Gorkha grief but also help present them in as solemn yet straightforward a way as possible, so that all the Gorkhas can understand and feel for them and, if possible, help improve their situation. If not, this would at least let them better prepare to face their problems for good.

The Gorkhas had a rough start from the very beginning. Life in the rugged mountains and hills was tough. The plains were full of mosquitos and overwhelmed by blistering heatwaves, thus unwelcoming and always fated with unkind, unfit, and cruel rulers. To be able to feed all the mouths at home, men had to walk for miles, face the cruelty of nature and humankind, and make themselves adapt to the laws of the new lands they found. As they adopted soldiering and farming as their means of living from the beginning, the journey took them initially both eastward and westward of Nepal, extending to Jammu and Kashmir to the west and Arunachal Pradesh and Nagaland to the east. They were just economic migrants trying to eke out two square meals a day without any malice or aspiration of their own that could harm their hosts. Besides, those hilly regions were their lands where their ancestors had roamed for centuries in search of a better life and suited their lifestyle. They did not cross the border; instead, these borders crossed them.

The Gorkhas have not had any good leaders throughout its history, and the 105 years of Rana's autocratic regime were its darkest days. These leaders did not allow education or reading to the public to prolong their ruthless rule, and levied heavy taxes on the people, leaving them with no choice but to flee to avoid starvation. The Gorkha institution that started in 1815 did not have any approval from the Ranas. As a result, the Ranas harassed the Gorkhas on their return home, confiscated their properties, and some were even killed as a punishment. When the Ranas realised the Gorkha's actual value, they started using the Gorkhas for their ulterior motives. Ranodhip Singh was the first Rana PM who sold the Gorkhas to the British for a rifle per head. Bir Shamsher sanctioned the first Gorkha enlistment policy to the British in 1886 to save his regime from Jagat Jung, Jang Bahadur's son and his legitimate rival. He had taken refuge in Benaras and needed a guarantee from the British that they would not side with Jagat Jung and claim power. Bir Shamsher sold the Gorkhas to keep himself and his family in power and helped establish the Gorkha institution that had become both boon and bane of the country for over two centuries.

With the Rana regime's seal of approval, the Gorkha institution swelled up to twenty battalions from just five before. It established itself as the most respected and potent Infantry Brigade within the British Indian Army. The Gorkha Brigade fought hard in every war and skirmish they had since then and played a pivotal role in the making of modern India. When the First World War struck, Chandra Shamsher broke all the limits and opened all the doors in Nepal for the British, sending over 200,000 Gorkhas out of its five million population to fight and die for the British—one in ten men did not return home. As if not to be outdone by history, Juddha Shamsher sent another 250,000 Gorkhas to the war. Virtually every able man from the country represented a staggering 20 per cent of the men out of its six million population, and over 33,300 Gorkhas, never made it home. In return for the Gorkha's services, the Ranas received a million rupees yearly until 1923. The British increased it to two million rupees after 1923, which went straight to the Prime Minister's private fund. With the deal, the Ranas benefited in more ways than one, killing two birds with a stone. Firstly, they received considerable money to enrich themselves and pay for their lavish lifestyle. Secondly, they did not have to deal with the Gorkhas, whom they had always considered troublemakers.

After India's independence in 1947, they (British, India and Nepal) signed a Tripartite Treaty regarding the continuity of the Gorkha's enlistment in the British and Indian Armies beyond that historical event. Unfortunately, the signing took place in a dubious manner where Padma Shamsher was allegedly taken to a separate room for a secret discussion with the British representative before he finally agreed to sign the treaty, and the repercussions of that betrayal could only be found many decades later. After seventy-five years, the Tripartite Treaty of 1947 has remained the only official paper currently regulating Gorkha's enlistment since then, even though many treaty provisions are no longer relevant and require urgent reviewing.

Just like their military cousins, the civilian side of the Gorkha communities, who were, in general, hill peasant cultivators, did not wait there and started emigrating both east and west of Nepal in masses. The main reason behind the mass migration was the deteriorating economic crisis due to the lack of cultivatable land, indebtedness, ecological crisis through intense cultivation and deforestation, growing population, heavy taxes, and the chronic shortage of food in the hill areas of central Nepal. The first migration started in the early nineteenth century, and by 1900, over 250,000 Gorkhas were said to have already been living in North India. As the British expanded their occupation and captured more new territories in Northeast India, they needed more workforce to administer the newly acquired lands. The Gorkhas were their readymade solutions. Either be it building new roads and railways, tending tea gardens and timber production, working in the oil and coal mines, guarding the administrative office compounds and the family quarters, or serving the sahibs and their memsahibs, the Gorkhas were always ready there to fill up all those vacancies. Those new frontier lands at the border with Myanmar and China were tribal areas, hence, scarcely populated and mostly covered with thick jungles, gorges, and swamps. To show who the boss around there was, the British needed to have some of their subjects physically living at the border areas, and they could not see anyone better suited than the Gorkhas to take up that vital role. Not to mention the sturdy Gorkha hands that needed to make it a cultivatable land by clearing out the thick jungles, ravines, and swamps of those inhospitable places. The Gorkhas moved in with their ever-expanding families and the cow herds, making the British a happy and relieved master.

As if putting their subjects under the darkness for 105 years was not already enough, Mohan Shamsher, the last Rana Prime Minister, did commit one last crime against its people by signing the Indo-Nepal Treaty 1950, and the Indian Gorkhas of Nepali origin are still paying the price for that mistake as of today. Especially cruel is Article 7 of the treaty, which allows an open border policy for both countries. It has turned out to be baneful to the Indian Gorkhas of Nepali origin, and the Gorkhas have been demanding the abolishment of the treaty since then. The Gorkha's problem might have been the last thing Mohan Shamsher had in his mind, for he only wanted to extend the Rana regime by agreeing with the new big guy in the region. History has indicated to us the Nepali rulers' willingness to compromise the well-being and interests of the people to stay in power and how much disregard and disrespect they had for their country and its citizens. They had used their people repeatedly to hang on the power and were more than willing to sacrifice them if necessary. At the end of the day, it's all about money, power, and position, and the Nepali leaders of the post-Rana era have yet to do much to prove otherwise. In short, it won't be an understatement if we say Nepali rulers played a significant role in aggravating the Gorkha grief and making their lives more miserable.

As described in previous chapters, the implications of the Gorkha institution in Nepal are massive and multi-layered. Socially, politically, economically, mentally, intellectually, communally, and emotionally, the Gorkha institution significantly impacts Nepal. Had it not been for the Gorkha institution, and the British, the landscape in Nepal might have been a lot different than it is today. Had it not been for the Gorkha institution, tens of thousands of Gorkhas would not have died in both WW1 and WW2 fighting somebody else's wars, tens of thousands of women would not have been widowed, and hundreds of thousands of children would not have been orphaned back at home. Just imagine the grief, pain, and anguish they have gone through and how the dreams and futures of those innocent people drowned in it. Had it not been for the Gorkha institution, the Gorkhas would not have to die in foreign countries such as Malaysia, Singapore, Borneo, Java, Hong Kong, the Falklands, Europe, Cyprus, Bosnia, Iraq, Afghanistan, and many others; they would not have had to become one among the unfortunate people who have graves in various countries around the world.

Had it not been for the Gorkha institution, people from the Janajaati (Gurung, Magar, Rai, Limbu, Sherpa, and Tamang) communities would have stayed back in Nepal, studied hard, competed with whatever they had in the country and made the best out of it. New generations would have occupied meaningful governmental offices, shared the duties and responsibilities of nation building, and contributed to the advancement and betterment of the people, community, and country. If not, Nepal would have at least avoided having such a lopsided community as it is today and stopped some particular communities from monopolising the power and position at the country's expense. Most importantly, all the children would have their fathers at their side as they grew, there would have been confidence and strong support for all the wives, and a strong pillar for all the families to always rely on bad and good days. Had it not been for the Gorkha institution, Nepal would have had normal families, a regular community, and a normal country-wide experience. Nepal may have still been a small and poor country, but at least it would have been dignified.

India has over a billion people. Why does it still need the Gorkhas to fight its wars and secure its borders? Nehru had no trust in the newly formed Indian army, for it had 60 per cent Muslims, and the Congress Party never trusted the Sikhs. In post-independent India, the Gorkhas were always at the forefront of the war, whether in Jammu and Kashmir, Hyderabad, the Sino-Indo war, the Sri Lankan crisis, or the three major Pakistan-India wars—you name it, and they were there. Had it not been for the Gorkhas at the borders and fighting India's wars, India would not have been where it is today, claiming itself as one of the world leaders as it would like to be called so much nowadays. And yet, instead of being grateful and respectful to the Gorkhas, why would they call them derogatory names like Chowkidar, Bahadur, or Kancha?

Had Nepal been strong, self-reliant, and acted like a sovereign country, India would have never treated Nepal like its own union state. Had Nepal ever gotten good and sensible leadership, they would have changed the Tripartite Treaty in 1947, and India would have stopped taking Gorkhas and Nepal for granted a long time ago. Had Mohan Shamsher not signed the Indo-Nepal Treaty of 1950 and introduced the open border policy, the Gorkhas would not have been displaced from the Northeast states of Assam, Meghalaya, Tripura, Mizoram, Manipur, Nagaland, and Arunachal Pradesh. Darjeeling and Kalimpong would not have cried for Gorkhaland, and Lhotshambas would not have fled Bhutan. Nepali youths from western Nepal would not have died crossing the single-wired makeshift bridge to India, and Nepali women would not have spent such hellish lives in brothels around the big cities of India. Had Nepal not been ruled by such a bunch of selfish, corrupted, useless, shameless, spineless sell-outs for so long, the Gorkhas would not have suffered such indignity and humiliation in India. After what they have done for India, the last thing the Gorkhas deserve is mockery, which says more about you than it does them, and therefore should be stopped immediately. If you cannot respect them, at least do not insult them.

In the post-Rana era, Nepal experienced many upheavals, including absolute monarchy, Panchayati one-party system, constitutional monarchy, multi-party system, communist uprising, abolishing the monarchy, and establishment of the federal republic. Yet, more was needed regarding the people's livelihood and the country's situation. After kicking the monarchy out, Nepal hoped for a modern, fair, capable ruler. Instead, they ended up with new leaders who turned out to be even corrupt, selfish, and morally rotten and had no concerns for the wellbeing of the public and country. All they cared for was power, money, and status, and they could do almost anything to remain in power. Within the last few decades, the country has plunged into such a point of no return where there are no jobs for its youths, zero industries, a nonexistent economy, no development, no rules of law, and nothing happens without bribes or connections. Nepal has become such a useless country that nothing happens without foreign aid, and its shameless elites have turned themselves into expert beggars.

Those new fake emperors have taken the country into such a dire condition that one only has to visit the Kathmandu valley once and see the condition of its streets. Signboards announcing their expertise and services on languages, skills, jobs, and opportunities in foreign countries are omnipresent and occupy almost every space on the roadside, buildings, and bridges. The offices of foreign embassies, INGOs, and institutions are almost everywhere, and one can hardly find a person who has no connection with any of them. One can also hardly find a student who wasn't attending a course or classes that had anything to do with their chance of securing a job outside the country. I met parents who could not wait for their children to become eighteen so they could send them outside. Even government officials, media, businesses, and other social corporations couldn't do a thing without foreign involvement, and I felt like the whole of Kathmandu Valley was working for the foreigners. What had become of this country? It has become a weak, poor, helplessly dependent country on the outside world.

Tens of thousands of Nepali youths go out of the country daily, and over six million Nepali youths work overseas at a time, making human resources the only export of the country that imports almost everything. A country surviving on remittance that imports twelve times its exports cannot hope for improvement anytime soon. The Gorkhas work in over a hundred countries around the globe and send money back home, earning a new name for themselves as the *New Lahures* as if the sufferings of the *old Lahures* were not embarrassing enough. It pains me to say this, but the Gorkhas situation has mostly stayed the same over the last two centuries. They relied on the outside before and still depend on the outside world even today. If their forefathers had fought in various parts of the world and sacrificed their lives for the sake of two square meals a day by then, their grandchildren are still doing the same today. I have seen enough Gorkhali youths working in inhumane situations in foreign countries.

The humiliation of working as illegal workers in a foreign country is not funny, for thousands of Gorkhas have worked illegally in war-torn places like Iraq and Afghanistan, and many have paid the ultimate price with their lives. How could one forget the gruesome killing of fourteen innocent Gorkhas by Iraqi militants called the army of Ansar Al-Sunna in 2004; 1400 Gorkhas lost their lives building those glittering football stadiums for the FIFA World Cup 2022 in Qatar alone, and many innocent youths have died working in other Gulf and Southeast Asian countries working in extreme conditions. Over ten thousand Gorkhas have been killed in the last decade alone, and the country received 4-5 dead bodies in coffins daily in Kathmandu airport. Those figures exclude workers who migrate through illegal channels and labourers who work in India. Suicide, traffic and work-related accidents, cardiac arrest, and other natural causes are the leading causes of death. They could have avoided this had the relevant authorities done their job correctly.

Being abused and tortured in Gulf nations, stripped to their underwear and beaten up like cattle in Malaysia, and used, mistreated, and exploited in India, these are all repetition in the suffering the Gorkhas regularly faced, as they can be easily found in social media in today's modern world. Working in dangerous situations, under extreme heat and the backbreaking conditions is the norm of the day for them. Being captured and tortured by foreign extremists is the risk they face and the chance of being dropped in the working place is more than a reality. In other words, the sufferings of the Gorkhas have continued for the last two hundred years, and the chances of lessening the Gorkha grief are almost zero to none, let alone eradicating them.

By 2017, Nepalis had migrated to 153 out of 193 (UN-recognised) countries and became one of the world's top manpower-exporting countries (in terms of size and population). I'm not sure whether to laugh or cry, though, to be honest. Migration has depleted the villages, turning them into empty, lonely, deserted places. There are no Gurungs in a Gurung village, no Magars in a Magar village, no Rais and Limbus in Rai and Limbu villages, and no Bahuns in a Bahun village. What's the use of those villages if the villagers have all left and turned their lands into soulless places? Nepali youths should be working for their people, villages, and the country. Nepali parents didn't raise their sons and daughters to be used, misused, and mistreated by other people.

Blaming others for your problems is easy, but that's not the solution. One must sort matters out within their homes before pointing fingers at others, and if one's house is in good order, united and strong, no outside force can shake it. Nepal had/has bad rulers; external factors also played a significant role in its fate. Yet most of the blame must be borne by the people, for they let this all happen and were ultimately responsible for Nepal's current situation. Too much time has been wasted, and it's about time the Nepali people start being serious and see the big picture. They must learn to stop talking, start working, be responsible, and understand the power of unity. They also must begin respecting themselves, their fellow compatriots, and the rules and regulations of the land. They must also know their value and love themselves, their people, and the country. They must learn to choose the right leader, stop being selfish and shortsightedness, and start believing in a strong and self-reliant nation. They must educate themselves, select between right and wrong, and know the importance of preserving one's history, heritage, tradition, culture, and way of life. Most importantly, they must be united, put the nation above anything else, and stop being sold out for cheap. They must know the importance and value of their vote.

A country is nothing more than a piece of land without its people, for it's the people who make a country rich, robust, and beautiful or lead it downwards, the other way around. Progress is the collective responsibility of the people of that particular country. At the same time, a person individually is nothing without a nation, for your identity and everything of your being is connected to your country. There needs to be more than just individual success or the success of a part of the community in this era of globalization; there is a vast international community out there, and one has to prove itself as good within the country as they are outside the country. Only then can the Gorkha people reduce the pain of the Gorkha grief they have been suffering so far and live the dignified life they deserve. The world already knows you guys as the brave of the braves; now you can start living as proud Gorkhas, too. All you need is a little confidence, belief in yourself, understanding of the importance of unity, don't be selfish and a sell-out, love yourself and your country, put your people, community and country above anything else, and give it your best. If every one of you from this beautiful country can come up together and start working towards this goal, the day of Nepal being one of the great nations of the world is not that far away. If not, I am afraid the Gorkha grief will have to continue for an uncertain future, which will be one of the saddest, most unfortunate and wasteful events in our history. And the new generations of Gorkha people must bear the responsibility for being the leading cause behind all that grief and failure.

As I have already said at the beginning, I didn't write this book to please or to offend any individual, community, or country but to tell the truth as it is. I was born and raised in a typical Gurung village in mid-western Nepal, where being the Gorkha was the only option the youth had. Like my grandfathers and uncles, I joined the British army at seventeen, went to Hong Kong, and never returned. Life has taken me to many countries, I have seen and dealt with various people, and have gained a general idea of how this world functions. Along the way, I also witnessed and experienced people's greed, selfishness, cruelty, ugliness, grief, discrimination, and misery. I was moved and saddened, especially by the hardship, pain, and suffering of the Gorkha people, and I was determined to compile and highlight their grief so my Gorkha people would learn from it and do something to improve it. They never should never to face the same fate that their forefathers suffered. The day my Gorkha people can live a simple, dignified, and honourable life without leaving their homes will be the happiest day of my life. That's all I want from the bottom of my heart for my fellow compatriots, and if this book can help me achieve that goal, I would take it as a job well done on my part, and I wish everyone all the best.

Acknowledgements

Without the support of these kind people, we wouldn't have this book, and I am grateful to each one of them from the bottom of my heart—thank you so much!

Kathmandu/Nepal: VK and Sushma Kunwar, Dr Ganesh Gurung, Losang Namgyal Rinpoche, Niraj B, Major (Retd) Dalman Goley, Major (Retd) Lalit Dewan, Manohar Yakthumba, Nishnuk Kthing, Dr Suresh Tamang, Dr Pratyush Onta, Jhalak Subedi, Amrit Gurung, Narayan Gurung, Chun Gurung, Ram Gurung, Lt Gen (Retd) Phatteh B. Limbu, Maj Gen (Retd) Ram B. Gurung, Capt (Retd) Harka Singh Thapa, DB Chetri and his son, LB Ghising, Bryan Hitan, Kumar Yatru, Dilu Gurung, Jai Gurung, Dr Hum Bahadur Gurung, and many more.

Dehradun: Lt Gen (Retd) Shakti and author Madhu Gurung, Capt (Retd) Prem Thapa, Col (Retd) Jeevan Chhetri, Bhupendra Karki, Pooja Subba, and the entire Gorkha Sudhar Sanga families.

Siliguri/Darjeeling/Kalimpong/Sikkim/Jalpaiguri: Raja Puniani Suraj Gurung, , the intellectual and political team, the Sainikpuri Gram Sewa Samiti, Suraj Sharma, Saakal Dewan, Hemant Pradhan, the political team, Dr Satyadeep Chhetri, Parshu Dahal, NB Khatiwada, the journalist and intellectual team at Gangtok, Sandip C. Jain, Manoj Bogati, the intellectual team, and many more.

Guwahati/Assam/Meghalaya: Bishal KC, Neeta Gurung, Nav and Munni Sapkota, Lil Bahadur Chhetri, and the people from Raid Marawat Nepali village, Meghalaya.

A special thank goes to Prof Mahendra P Lama, Prof Vimal Khawas, Maj Gen. (Retd) Gopal Gurung, Lt Col (Retd) JP Cross, Kanak Mani Dixit, Prof Ela Sharma, Prof Suresh Dhakal, Prof Ramesh Dhungel, Dr Sanjeev Upreti and Ms Archana Thapa, Prof Janak Rai, Prof Neeti Aryal Khanal, Dr Bekh Bahadur Thapa and Dr Rita Thapa, Dr Yubaraj Sangraula, Sudheer Sharma, Pranaya Rana, Purna Basnet, Gajendra Budhathoki, Deepak Prakash Bhatt, and many more.

Thanks to Tirtha Gurung bhai for being with me during our India trip and to Prem Gurung bhai and the entire family for your hospitality during our trip to Sikles and other regional Gurung villages.

I am grateful to my publisher, Renu Kaul Verma, editor Anuradha Mukherjee, the editorial team, the cover designer, and everyone involved in making this book a reality at Vitasta Publishing. I am also grateful to my friend Rashmi Ranjan Parida for his support.

Special thanks to my brother-in-law Rajendra Gurung, for caring for me during my stay in Kathmandu. I am incredibly grateful and indebted to my dearest wife, Tina Gurung, and to my son and daughter, for their unwavering support and encouragement. You know how much I love you, and it would have been impossible without your support and encouragement. Thank you so much!

–Tim I Gurung